Living Through History

THE ROARING TWENTIES:

BRITAIN IN THE 1920s

GRAHAM MITCHELL

B. T. Batsford Ltd London

ACKNOWLEDGMENTS

The Author and Publishers would like to thank the following for their kind permission to reproduce copyright illustrations: BBC Hulton Picture Library for figures 3, 4, 5, 7, 10, 12, 15, 16, 20, 23, 37, 45, 46, 50 and 60; The Cherwell (A.D. Peters) for figure 17; Condé Nast Publications for figure 30; Mary Evans Picture Library for the frontispiece and figures 1, 14 and 41; Dr David Hodgson for figure 53; Mandel Archive for figure 27; the Raymond Mander and Joe Mitchenson Theatre Collection for figures 19, 21 and 22; The Mansell Collection for figures 2, 6, 8, 13, 28, 40, 43, 44, 48, 56 and 59; National Portrait Gallery for figure 52; Plymouth City Museum and Art Gallery for figure 58; Popperfoto for figures 29, 54 and 57; Reresby Sitwell for figure 39; Sotheby's London (Cecil Beaton photograph) for figures 24 and 26; Marie Stopes House for figures 49 and 51; the Tate Gallery for figures 32, 35 and 36; H. Roger Viollet for figure 25; the Wyndham Lewis Trust for figures 33 and 34. Photographs 9, 11 and 42 are from the Batsford Archives. The pictures were researched by Patricia Mandel.

COVER ILLUSTRATIONS

The colour photograph shows a fashionable golfing party (Mary Evans Picture Library); the black and white print shows a Poor Relief soup kitchen (BBC Hulton Picture Library); the portrait is of Nancy Cunard (Cecil Beaton photograph, courtesy of Sotheby's London).

First published 1986

ISBN 0 7134 5201 3

Printed in Great Britain by
R J Acford
Chichester, Sussex
for the publishers
Batsford Academic and Educational,
an imprint of B.T. Batsford Ltd,
4 Fitzhardinge Street
London W1H 0AH

Frontispiece
Cocktails were all the rage at parties in the Twenties (*Mary Evans Picture Library*).

CONTENTS

The Illustrations

The Twenties

1 In the Twenties leisure activities and sports were enjoyed by an increasingly large number of people. Golf and tennis became especially popular.

Of all the decades of the twentieth century the Twenties is the one which conjures up the most vivid, colourful and vibrant images. In the popular imagination it is the "Jazz Age", "The Roaring Twenties", a time of gaiety and liberation from the shackles of the past, of youthful frivolity and excess. And it is true that the Twenties was the first era in history when the younger generation felt that they held the centre of the social stage, by right, having survived the carnage of the First World War. They were determined, in Noël Coward's phrase, to "have themselves a ball!"

The older generation, in general, looked on with grave disapproval, shocked by what it considered to be irresponsible, immature and immoral behaviour. However, whether they liked it or not, most accepted that the old order had changed, yielding place to new. The sober, traditional values of the late Victorian and Edwardian period had been blown to bits on the battlefields of the Somme and Passchendaele. To many young people the values of their fathers' generation had been seen to be empty platitudes, which had led only to slaughter and destruction. After the First World War life could never be the same again.

This spirit of rebellion and liberation from the past shown by the young was expressed in everything they said, wore or did. As Susanne Everett in *London: The Glamorous Years 1919–1930* comments:

Gone were the stuffy conventions and hide-bound rules that had governed polite society before the war. Carefully arranged piled-up hair, hour-glass figures, whalebone corsets, wine-cup and the waltz had been replaced by the 'bob', loose clothes, dry martinis, the tango and the shimmy-shake. Young men and women danced together cheek to cheek with shameless abandon, women were seen smoking Egyptian cigarettes through long ivory holders, or driving themselves in smart open-air roadsters, small round felt hats pulled down over their eyes.

The fashions of the Twenties were as much the outward expression of an ethical as an aesthetic idea; they symbolized the new-found freedom and independence of a whole generation, and most particularly, of women. The emphasis was on comfort and convenience: the "modern girl" of the Twenties nicknamed a "flapper", wore her hair and her hemline short; she threw away her corsets (rather as in the Seventies girls burnt their bras) and wore camisoles and camiknickers; she strapped her bust to achieve a slimline boyish look; she smoked, drank and drove fast cars. As far as she was concerned the past was dead: now it was a case of "Long Live The Present!"

And "living for the present" meant having fun. As Carolyn Hall comments in *The Twenties in Vogue*:

People made up for lost time with a frenzy of night-time gaiety. 'Our books, our clothes, our life, as our music, grow each year more syncopated' wrote Vogue in 1925. From America came the pulsating jazz rhythms and the dances to do to them: the foxtrot, one-step, Charleston, Black Bolton, Blues, tap-dancing. The Charleston, especially, became an obsession. Santos Casani demonstrated it on top of a taxi driven through London's West End and vicars declared it an offence against womanly purity. Noël Coward summed up the empty restlessness of the age in his lyrics 'Dance, Little Lady' (1928):

Tho' you're only seventeen
Far too much of a life you've seen
Syncopated child.
Maybe if you only knew
Where your path was leading to
You'd become less wild.
But I know it's vain
Trying to explain,
While there's this insane
Music in your brain

2 Comfort replaced contours in the Twenties. Loose-fitting clothes (and underclothes) replaced the laced and corsetted fashions of the Edwardian period.

3 Bee Jackson, the world champion Charleston dancer from the United States, kicking up her heels.

The music of the Twenties was like "a fever in the blood", as vital as it was frivolous and superficial: the energy of its rhythms animated a whole generation, from shopgirls to the Prince of Wales (who was himself a keen dancer, proud of his prowess at the Charleston).

The Twenties was an era of "crazes": everyone was forever on the look-out for novelties and new sensations. Among the most popular were pogo sticks, crossword puzzles, auction bridge, yo-yos, bananas, mah-jong, bathing beauty contests, potato crisps, cocktails and anything and everything Egyptian (after the opening of Tutankhamen's tomb by Lord Caernarvon in 1923). Sports like golf and tennis became immensely popular, both with men and women. The motor-car revolutionized people's attitude to travel: speed came to matter as much if not more than accessibility. The Twenties was an

4 Smoking – in private or in public – became a popular habit among "emancipated" women. Cigarette-holders, often long-stemmed and slim, were very much in vogue.

era of rapid change: it was a "fast" decade, running away from the black nightmare of the First World War but uncertain of its destination, or even its direction.

For perhaps the first time in history a whole generation looked across the Atlantic to America for its inspiration. As Carolyn Hall observes,

> A steady stream of songs, cocktails, expressions, films and entertainers flowed eastwards across the Atlantic and were snapped up with relish. (*The Twenties in Vogue*)

There was also a steady stream of American heiresses happy to trade their wealth for an aristocratic European title: they brought with them their own brand of New World vivacity and disregard for convention.

5 Gala Day at the new Thames resort at Hampton Court. The modern fashion for more revealing swimwear very much in evidence.

American films (made in the studios of Hollywood) quickly became the most popular form of entertainment in Britain. Charlie Chaplin, Rudolph Valentino, Mary Pickford, Douglas Fairbanks, Greta Garbo, and a host of other film "stars" were soon household names, worshipped as idols by men, women, and children who flocked in their thousands to the new picture-houses which sprang up all over the country.

And always, and seemingly everywhere, in the background the insistent sound of the songs and dances of the "Jazz Age", probably America's most influential export in the Twenties.

If you had money, and preferably social position, and were eager to enjoy a life of hedonistic self-indulgence then the Twenties was a time of seemingly unlimited opportunities to indulge your whims and fantasies. It was the decade of the "Bright Young People" (or "Bright Young Things") as they were dubbed by a press avid for scandal and sensa-

tion (and, naturally, shocked to discover it!). The Bright Young People were the children of wealthy and aristocratic families (primarily centred on London's Mayfair), who delighted in turning their backs on the conventional social life of their parents and indulging in often wild and reckless, but always pleasure-seeking, behaviour. They had a passion for dressing-up: fancy-dress parties, often wildly extravagant in conception, proliferated all over London, with the Bright Young People always to the forefront.

Evelyn Waugh in his satirical novel *Vile Bodies* lists a few of the more bizarre party-ideas:

> Masked parties, Savage parties, Victorian parties, Greek parties, Wild West parties, Russian parties, Circus parties, parties where one had to dress as somebody else, almost naked parties in St John's Wood, parties in flats and studios and houses and ships and hotels and night-clubs, in windmills and swimming baths . . .

Though *Vile Bodies* is a work of fiction all these parties had actually taken place, and many more besides. The swimming bath party had been thrown by, amongst others, Brian Howard, who was always one of the prime inspirers of the Bright Young People's most extravagant behaviour.

Cocktails were all the rage at parties in the Twenties. As Alan Jenkins in *The Twenties* observes,

> One great symbol of the Twenties or 'Cocktail Age' was the grinning barkeep, in white mess jacket, athletically operating his cocktail shaker . . . at home the cocktail cabinet joined the phonograph and the radio as articles of furniture.

The craze soon spread to most sections of society, though it is doubtful if many cocktails were shaken or stirred in the industrial north where unemployment made even a pint of beer a luxury for many men. In the Twenties the fads and fancies of the wealthy were rapidly "taken up" by the less privileged: it was an age of almost instant popularization.

It was also an age of instant mass-production. In the Twenties the first British mass-produced cars were coming off the assembly lines: by the end of the decade the Morris Minor and the "baby" Austin brought the chance of car ownership to the masses. The advent of "off-the-peg" clothes, for both men and women, brought a degree of fashion-consciousness to most sections of society: fashions and styles created by the smart set rapidly became the property of the general public. Advertising became an increasingly important industry, as the value of the new, wider market for consumer goods became obvious. Large-scale multiple stores, such as Woolworth's and Marks and Spencer's, sprang up all over the country, replacing the old-fashioned family-run shops. The process was one of levelling out; "more cheaper goods for the many" was almost the slogan of the times.

6 Advertising became all the rage

7 Ex-servicemen singing to a West End theatre queue, an all too familiar sight throughout the decade.

For some, however, even the cheapest goods were too expensive. In the immediate post-war period the return of huge numbers of servicemen to civilian life led to widespread unemployment in Britain, but by the winter of 1920 the vast majority had been reabsorbed into the nation's workforce. For a time industry boomed. However, this artifically fuelled bubble of prosperity soon burst, and it became increasingly obvious that the evil of unemployment would be an ever-present social reality throughout the post-war years. By June of 1921 two and a half million people were unemployed and, though this was a peak in the early Twenties, the figure never fell below a million throughout the decade.

If the Twenties was for some a time of gaiety for a depressingly large percentage of the population it was time of hardship and the struggle to avoid destitution and starvation. To many of the men who had returned from the trenches in 1918 the promise of "a land fit for heroes" must have seemed like a grim joke.

If you were out of work you drew the dole, which was fifteen shillings a week for a family of five. Alternatively you hired a barrel-organ and played it in the street, wearing your war-medals, with a chalked notice which said 'Ex-serviceman, wife and five kids to support'. (Alan Jenkins, *The Twenties*)

The heroic status of the returned servicemen did not last long, as Irene Clephanne in *We Ourselves 1900–1930* drily records:

Within two years of the cessation of fighting the men who had fought – for whom nothing was to be too good – underwent transformation in the popular middle-class imagination into lazy good-for-nothings of revolutionary tendencies whose sole idea was to avoid work and live on the 'dole'.

The old class suspicions and hostilities, forgotten or set aside in the camaraderie of the trenches, were soon revived and even strengthened (the Russian Revolution had been a sobering and chastening experience for the "owning" classes in Britain).

Industrial and agricultural over-production exacerbated the problem: prices, which had begun to fall in 1921, continued to decline at an accelerating pace but purchasers in sufficient numbers could not be found for goods and produce either at home or abroad. Corn, coffee, cotton, wool, fruit, meat were left to rot, burnt, or thrown into the sea. Britain's major industries foundered. Irene Clephanne again points to the absurdity of what was happening:

> Cupidity and stupidity had combined to bring about a ludicrous situation in which, in a world chock-full of unsold goods of all kinds, millions of men, women and children were creeping about underfed, bootless and clad in rags. (*We Ourselves 1900–1930*)

In 1923 what would have seemed impossible only a few years before happened: a Labour government, pledged to implement socialist policies, took office (backed by the ailing Liberal Party). For the nation's underprivileged this offered the hope of a new deal. But Ramsay MacDonald, the first Labour prime minister, once the euphoria had died down, found himself facing almost insuperable problems, and his administration, for all its good intentions, could do little to reverse the economic trend downwards or improve the lot of the low-paid and unemployed. MacDonald and his colleagues were profoundly embarrassed by their failure to help the very people who had helped to bring them to power, and some must have felt almost relieved when in November 1923, exactly ten months after they took office, their administration was toppled when the Liberals, who held the balance of power, withdrew their support. By the time a second Labour administration was formed, in 1929, again under the leadership of Ramsay MacDonald, Britain had experienced another first – the first ever general strike in its history – and was going through a slump more starkly precipitous than that which MacDonald had left behind in 1923.

The intervening six years had been years of economic depression and strife, presided over by the moderate, accommodating, but determined proponent of constitutional law, Stanley Baldwin. Baldwin and his Conservative government did not lack compassion for the human victims of the nation's economic difficulties but they were themselves the victims of world economic forces which they were unable to control. When in 1925 Britain returned to the Gold Standard, hoping to achieve financial stability, the situation worsened. Particularly badly hit were the mine-owners, and when, later in 1925, the Government announced that it would have to end its subsidy to the coal industry, the embattled mine-owners announced plans to reduce wages, abolish the minimum wage principle, and enforce longer hours on their workforce – i.e. more work for less pay!

The miners, backed by the railwaymen, threatened a nationwide strike. The govern-

8 The first Labour Prime Minister: a fine orator and astute politician, committed to social reform, who found himself unable to find solutions to the problems of large-scale unemployment and social deprivation which bedevilled the inter-war years.

ment immediately commissioned an enquiry under Judge Sankey to assess the rights and wrongs of the dispute: it came out in favour of the mine-owners. Subsidies to the mining industry were condemned and it was recommended that hours should stay the same, and wages be cut. The incensed miners, on 26 April 1926, stopped work. Determined and defiant they came up with their own slogan: "Not a minute on the day: not a penny off the pay". The General Council of the Trades Union Congress met and pledged itself and its members to back the miners' cause. A historic confrontation became inevitable when the government refused to enter into negotiations with the miners' leaders for fear of displaying weakness. The T.U.C. leaders then announced that they would call a general strike at midnight on 3 May unless, by then, negotiations had started. The appointed hour came and went, and the General Strike began.

Stanley Baldwin's government was less disquieted than the T.U.C. leaders expected them to be. To the government the General Strike offered an opportunity to slay the dragon of growing union power once and for all. If for the trades unionists the General Strike was a struggle to retain essential rights and freedoms, for those ranged against them it was a struggle against the forces of anarchy and disorder. As it was the dragon roared for only ten days, then (with the exception of the miners) once more bowed its head to the yoke.

During the ten days of the General Strike many jobs and essential services were carried out by volunteers from the middle and upper classes. Inflamed by jingoistic patriotism and spurred on by a desire to "put the lower orders in their place" many a wealthy Lord and his Lady cut a biazarre figure at the wheel of a London omnibus or a milk lorry. For them it was all tremendous fun. Amongst the willing eager volunteers who flocked to "do their bit" were busloads of "plus-four boys" from public schools and universities who volunteered for driving buses and trains. As Alan Jenkins records in *The Twenties*, some unusual destination boards were to be seen on London buses, such as:

This bus goes anywhere you like. No fares and kind treatment. Joy rides to the East End.

or:

The driver of this bus is a student of Guy's Hospital. The conductor is a student of Guy's. Anyone who interferes with either is liable to be a patient of Guy's.

It all ended disappointingly quickly for some. Loelia Ponsonby remembers,

Quite frankly, my friends and I were amused by the novelty and excitement of the strike, and it was over before it had time to pall.

For the trades unionists defeat was a bitter, humiliating pill to swallow. They had accepted a face-saving formula presented to them by the Chairman of the Coal Commission, promising a further temporary subsidy for the coal industry, but only because it had become clear that the General Strike could only end in disaster for the trades union movement if prolonged. The miners themselves refused the compromise "solution" and remained firmly obdurate for a further six months till hardship and hunger finally drove them to surrender and return to work.

The ramifications of the failure of the General Strike were felt throughout the industrial areas of Britain, and are still felt today.

The complete humiliation of the working man in his greatest bid to redress the imbalance of the old society, in his greatest moment of risk-taking, was seen by the ruling class as total triumph, but the ugly and cruel defeat of the General Strike has left a legacy of bitterness between bosses and workers that is with us still. (Marina Walker, *The Crack in the Tea Cup*)

What the General Strike had signally failed to do was to better the lot of the low-paid or the unemployed. Poverty and hardship increased as the decade wore on: the abject failure of the General Strike seemed to knock the stuffing out of those who had sought

9 During the General Strike of 1926 a special Civil Constabulary group was set up to deal with potential confrontations or riots. Here they are seen leaving their buses on the day the General Strike collapsed.

radically to change British society. The zeal for revolutionary change was replaced by widespread apathy. While the Bright Young Things capered in Mayfair and those with money enough in their pockets to pay for an evening out danced the night away, the dark clouds of The Depression grew darker by the month. By the time the new decade dawned there was little left for anybody to sing about and still less to dance about.

The gloom and despondency which was to characterize the first half ot the new decade was already the prevailing national mood. If Bright Young Things enjoying a seemingly endless party is the image of the Twenties which people prefer to retain, it should always be remembered that the reality of the Twenties for many at the foot of the social ladder was closer to the image associated by most people with the Thirties – that of groups of men in cloth caps standing forlornly on street corners . . . the men had been gathering, like swallows with nowhere to go, throughout the Roaring Twenties. For them the Twenties had never roared, and though they never made the news, except as statistics, their experience of life in the Britain of the Twenties is as valid a document of the times as that of their more illustrious contemporaries.

10 A poor relief soup kitchen for the homeless and unemployed, 1924.

High Society

In the immediate post-war period the old-established families who had dominated London society and dictated conventions of dress and behaviour found themselves out of step with the prevailing mood of the times. They wanted to re-establish the status quo which had existed before the war, but people were no longer prepared to accept the old ways of doing things.

Fashionable society in the Twenties was a lively, cosmopolitan, international mixture of men and women from widely differing backgrounds and spheres of activity. As Carolyn Hall observes:

Dukes' daughters married commoners and actresses married peers. (*The Twenties in Vogue*)

The old conventions were flagrantly ignored by members of the smart set, who openly scorned the rigid, constricting social attitudes of the older generation. A spirit of modernity was in the air, inspired by the behaviour and approach to life of the most influential trend-setter of the decade, the Prince of Wales, who, almost single-handed, rewrote the rules of what was acceptable in "polite society". His father, King George V, fretted and fumed, but the Prince continued to go his own way regardless, the living embodiment of his generation's sense of emancipation from the past.

Parties soon replaced formal dinners as the fashionable way to entertain (though many of the older generation continued to honour the old ways). Top of the list of society party-givers were the rich American expatriates, Laura Corrigan and Elsa Maxwell. Laura Corrigan first popularized "cabaret" parties, which rapidly became a feature of Twenties social life. Instead of taking her guests to a restaurant to see a cabaret, she brought the atmosphere of the restaurant, and the cabaret, to them. She also popularized the practice of holding tombola games at her parties, the prizes ranging from Cartier gold cigarette cases to more humble silver pencils, the best prizes always going to the wealthiest and most influential guests. Of the many English society hostesses Lady Colefax, Syrie Maugham (the estranged wife of Somerset Maugham) and Mrs Henry Maclaren were

11 Revellers in fancy dress at the 1924 Empire Ball, held in the Albert Hall.

the most successful and popular, the rivalry between Lady Colefax and Syrie Maugham being a subject of gossip throughout the decade.

Invitations to Lady Emerald Cunard's parties and dinners were greatly prized by the more literate and articulate, and Lady Londonderry reigned supreme as the First Lady of the political salons (an assertion which would doubtless have been challenged by Lady Desborough, Lady Wimborne or the irrepressible Nancy, Lady Astor).

First spotted, and "taken up" by Lady Colefax, Noël Coward rapidly became a "must" on every self-respecting society hostess's guest list. By the end of the decade he was occupying centre stage in smart society circles. "Everyone who was anyone" laughed at his wit, sang his songs and imitated his style of dress and speech.

Not all the children of the denizens of "high" society in the Twenties were content to dance away the decade without a serious thought in their heads: for some the bohemian life associated with writers and artists held a strong attraction. Someone who seemed to bridge the two worlds was Nancy Cunard, who for many people was the epitome of the "modern woman", with her carefree fecklessness and love of night-life, but who was herself happiest living *la vie bohémienne*, surrounded by the artists, writers and intellectuals of the Latin Quarter in Paris.

Though many of the old, time-honoured events on the social calendar continued as before (such as Ascot, Henley and the debutantes' "coming out" balls) the Twenties saw society loosening its stays, and opening its dusty doors. There were losses as well as gains: the old social order, though riddled with snobbery and class-consciousness, stood for certainty in the midst of uncertainty, security in the midst of insecurity. The post-war generation had much to prove: regrettably, for the most part, the men and women who had the wealth and influence to assist in the fashioning of a new social order were content merely to order a new social fashion.

The Prince of Wales (1894–1972)

Edward Albert Christian George Andrew Patrick David, the eldest son of King George V and Queen Mary and, consequently, the Prince of Wales, was in every way a man of his times. As Stella Margetson in *The Long Party* notes:

> For millions of the young of all classes everywhere the slight figure of the Prince of Wales very soon became a symbol of their longing and their determination to break away from the stuffiness of the old world into the air and the daylight of the new.

The contrast in attitudes and interests between the Prince and his father was clear from an early age: it became more pronounced as Prince Edward (or David, as he was known within the royal family) grew into a young man determined not to be straight-jacketed by what he considered to be outmoded and inhibiting habits of dress, behaviour and thought. He belonged to a generation which had endured the carnage of the Western Front: he had himself "supp'd full of horrors" as a serving officer in the trenches. He recognized what his father never could bring himself to accept – that the old pre-war world of Edwardian attitudes and values was dead. A new approach was needed to respond to a new age, especially where the royal family was concerned: rejecting the aloof, dignified paternalism of his father, he determined to go out and "meet the people".

In the early Twenties, with his father's uneasy blessing, he went out and met the people all over the British Empire and beyond. Described by one contemporary journalist as "the Empire's travelling salesman", he journeyed indefatigably, and with seemingly boundless energy and vitality, achieving enormous popularity wherever he went. Between 1919 and 1923 he travelled over 100,000 miles round the world by sea and land, representing his country's interests.

His first trip abroad, in 1919 set the tone for the rest: on a whistle-stop tour of Canada he travelled the length and breadth of the country, constantly stopping to make speeches, attend functions, shake hands and chat to as many people as he could. The Canadians loved him both as a prince and as a man prepared to participate and not simply observe. At Nipigon he "roughed it" for several days with local Indians; at Saskatoon he mounted a bronco at a rodeo . . . and kept his seat, much to the onlookers' delight. The tour was an immense success. To his father's disquiet he ended it by crossing over the border to America, where a nation of arch-republicans found themselves idolizing a prince of the blood royal. Commenting on the Prince's remarkable popularity one writer for a leading American newspaper spoke for the nation:

It's the smile of him, the unaffected modest bearing of him, the natural fun-loving spirit that twinkles in his blue eyes, and that surest of all poses, the recognition of duty to be done triumphing over a youngster's natural unease and embarrassment.

12 The Prince of Wales, surrounded by admirers, outside the Ontario Agricultural College on his trip to Canada in 1919. He was immensely popular wherever he went.

The American press made the maximum capital out of the Prince's popularity. One magazine ran a competition in which readers were invited to "write a love-letter to the Prince of Wales!" Twenty bags of mail soon piled up in the editor's office. The Prince himself, if modestly embarrassed by such excesses, was delighted by the frankness, spontaneity and humour of the American people: thereafter he always felt at home there.

Further tours followed. In March 1920, he was off on his travels to New Zealand and Australia, calling in on the Carribean Islands *en route*. Once again his receptions were rapturous: the normally suspicious Australians in particular loved his naturalness and spontaneous friendliness. The *Sydney Sun* put it succintly:

> Before the Prince landed, the popular idea of princes was of something haughty and remote; but this smiling, appealing, youthful man smiled away the difference which Australians believed lay between Royalty and the common people.

13 The Prince, photographed in Delhi during his controversial visit to India in 1921–2, his full-dress military regalia as solemnly ceremonial as his expression.

When he finally sailed from Sydney he had visited every state and shaken so many hands that his right hand was too sore and stiff to use – so he used his left. Affectionately, the Australians nicknamed him the "Digger".

Returning to England he was permitted a year's rest before his next trip, this time to India. He boarded ship for what was to prove his most taxing and strenuous tour in November 1921. It was not a propitious time for such a visit: two years before General Dyer, the Commander in Chief of British forces in India, had ordered British troops to open fire on unarmed Indian civilians to quell a riot, killing nearly 400 people. Gandhi's Congress party was growing increasingly influential and disruption and ill-will was predicted. Commentators who understood Indian politics feared the worst. However, whatever his private feelings about the visit, and he was less than enthusiastic about it, the Prince set out to win friends and restore confidence. After an initial triumph with the Maratha tribesmen at Poona, the Prince scarcely put a foot wrong, delighting crowds wherever he went, and handling Indian dignitaries with tact and understanding. Despite the Congress party's opposition he was boycotted only twice on the whole tour, at Lucknow and Allahabad. He seemed to have the gift of making all Indians, from every social stratum, feel he took an interest in them.

When he returned home he was greeted by cheering crowds in London. Even his father, so often critical of his eldest son's behaviour, felt moved to praise him. His popularity seemed universal.

So much for the public figure, the idol of his generation. What of the private man? His cousin, Lord Louis Mountbatten, who toured Australasia and India alongside the Prince wrote, many years later:

> I soon realised that under the delightful smile which charmed people everywhere, and despite all the fun we managed to have, he was a lonely and sad person, always liable to deep depressions.

In his autobiography *A King's Story*, published in 1957, the Prince, by then the Duke of Windsor, reflected on the nature of his official duties:

> Lonely drives through tumultuous crowds, the almost daily inspection of serried ranks of veterans, the inexhaustible supply of cornerstones to be laid, the commemorative trees to be planted . . . sad visits to hospital wards, every step bringing me face to face with some inconsolable tragedy . . . always more hands to shake than a dozen Princes could have coped with.

The picture of a young man prone to melancholia, prematurely weighed down with the responsibilities of his position, which emerges from such comments seems impossible to reconcile with the public's view of him. And yet, in a sense, it may help to explain it. Throughout the Twenties, much to his father's disapproval, the Prince was constantly to be seen enjoying the life of a young man-about-town. Popular with women, he lived a full and active social life. A habitué of the better class of night-club he was frequently to be found at the fashionable Embassy Club in Bond Street, dancing the night away (generally in the company of the separated Mrs Dudley Ward with whom he shared a close relationship for 17 years). In the daytime he indulged in a wide variety of sports, including tennis, golf and steeplechasing (until his father put a ban on his participation in such a dangerous sport after a near-fatal accident). Like so many of his generation he lived life at speed (he had a passion for fast cars), almost as though he distrusted the future – or feared it. Perhaps it is not too fanciful to suggest that he sought an escape from his "dark moods" in the bright effervescent world of the London clubland of the Twenties.

His father could see little excuse for it, however, and wrote in a letter to a confidant:

> I see David continues to dance every night and most of the night. People who don't know him will begin to think that he is either mad or the biggest rake in Europe. Such a pity.

14 The Embassy Club, in Bond Street, a favourite night-spot of the Prince's, where he was frequently to be seen in the company of the Hon. Mrs Dudley Ward, a close friend of his throughout the Twenties.

In thinking this the King was wrong: few saw him as anything other than a young man expressing a healthy reassertion of life after the grim horrors of the First World War. And, moreover, to the vast majority of British people he seemed, for all his excesses, a man whose basic instincts were humane and generous.

What perhaps more than anything else endeared him to them was the obvious sincerity of his distress at the worsening state of industrial relations in the country, with its concomitant bitter strikes leading to poverty, hardship and increasing unemployment. Since the end of the war the young Prince had taken a deep, personal interest in the welfare of working men, and in particular ex-servicemen with whom he felt a special kinship. He actively supported the Rev. Tubby Clayton's Christian organization Toc H, and the newly founded British Legion, a society pledged to serve the interests of ex-servicemen throughout the world.

"I feel more at home with the Legion than anywhere else", he once said, and the majority of his fellow-countrymen believed him, and respected him for it. As the great depression of the late Twenties began to bite, bringing huge armies of unemployed men and undernourished children on to the street corners of the industrial North and the Welsh valleys, the Prince redoubled his efforts to relieve some of their misery and suffering. He travelled seemingly incessantly to the worst-hit areas, tirelessly fund-raising to help alleviate the hardship. What he saw in the industrial slums shocked him profoundly.

> Some of the things I see in their gloomy, poverty-stricken areas make me almost ashamed to be an Englishman. Isn't it awful that all I can do is make them smile?

In 1928 he became patron of the National Council of Social Service and directed the energies of this organization into working on behalf of the unemployed: thousands of volunteers were recruited to help find opportunities for recreation and useful occupation for unemployed men and women. The Prince's work for the Coalfields Distress Fund moved even the fiery and truculent leader of the miners, A. J. Cook, to comment:

> We owe to the Prince a real measure of thanks . . . he has proved to the miner and his children at a moment of great suffering and distress that they are not forgotten.

If the Prince in the Twenties was to some the Playboy Prince, he was, to others, the Prince Who Cared.

Throughout the decade he continued his overseas tours: in 1923 he visited Belgium to unveil the war memorial to the British dead; in 1924 he returned to the United States; in 1925 he toured West Africa and South Africa, and, later, South America; in 1927 he revisited Canada to attend the Diamond Jubilee Celebration of the Canadian Confederation; finally, in 1928 he visited East Africa . . . only to have the tour cut short when news of his father's grave illness reached him in Tanganyika.

15 The Prince talking to wounded ex-servicemen at Tottenham in the summer of 1923; he always retained a special place in his affections for the victims of the war years.

The King recovered but his illness left him weakened and easily tired: the Prince of Wales had to face the fact that he might ascend to the throne at any time. Though he retained his popularity with the vast majority of the British public, to the end of the Twenties and into the Thirties, some people, particularly politicians, had doubts about his ability to fulfil his duties as a monarch. They recognized his good qualities, but were troubled by the hint of callowness and immaturity in his temperament which could, on occasions, lead to irresponsibly self-indulgent behaviour. He could be obstinate and at times opinionated.

He finally ascended to the throne in January 1936. When, the following December, he chose to abdicate in order to marry the woman he loved, the divorcee Wallis Simpson, the sense of shock felt by the British people was echoed throughout the Empire and beyond. He sailed into what turned out to be a lifetime of exile, leaving behind only memories of the years during which he had been one of the most popular men in the world.

Brian Howard (1905–58)

To many, the brightest star in the galaxy of Bright Young People who enlivened the Twenties' social scene was the Etonian dandy, homosexual and self-proclaimed aesthete, Brian Howard.

The son of American parents, Brian Howard was sent to a well-known preparatory school in 1913, where he later claimed to have been seduced by one of his masters, and went on to Eton in 1918. From the outset of his career at Eton Brian Howard set out to make an impression.

His early years there passed without too much incident: he achieved considerable popularity, and some notoriety, by making the most of his good looks in the traditional public school manner. He clearly "made an impression" on his housemaster, who, in 1921, wrote to Brian's mother:

16 Brian Howard.

> It has seldom been my lot, in many years of work amongst boys, to come upon one so entirely self-centred and egotistical . . . so far as his moral nature is concerned I cannot find what standards he has other than those of pure selfishness . . .

Fortunately not all his teachers saw him in quite so unfavourable a light. One who recognized his precocious flair for literature and poetry was Aldous Huxley, then a young teacher at Eton. By 1921, a key year in his life, Brian had become a passionate lover, and champion, of Modernism in the arts in general, and poetry in particular. He was encouraged in this by Edith Sitwell, one of the leaders of the Modernist movement in English poetry, to whom he had sent some Dadaist poems that he had written. She wrote:

Dear Mr Howard. There can be not the slightest doubt that your gifts and promise are exceedingly remarkable. You are undoubtedly what is known as a 'born writer' . . . I see more remarkable talent and promise in your work than in that of any other poet under twenty I have seen (excepting that of my brother Sacheverell) . . .

Such immoderate praise confirmed Brian in his view of himself as a young man of immense promise as a writer. To bring this fact to the attention of a wider audience he decided to produce his own literary magazine. This he did in 1922 with the help of his friend (and rival) a fellow dandy and aesthete, Harold Acton. The magazine, produced on shocking pink paper with bright yellow end-papers, was called *The Eton Candle*. Though the two editors themselves wrote the bulk of the magazine's prose and poetry, a number of leading young contemporary writers who had already achieved critical recognition were persuaded to contribute, including Aldous Huxley and Osbert and Sacheverell Sitwell.

For a "school magazine" the *Eton Candle* received unprecedented review coverage, including reviews in *The Times Literary Supplement* and the *Morning Post*. Letters of congratulation flooded in to the editors: even their critics at Eton were forced, grudgingly, to recognize their achievement. Brian was cock-a-hoop: not only had he "made an impression" at Eton, but he had also received attention (much of it favourable) from the larger world of literature and the arts. He ended his time at Eton confident that he would soon achieve recognition as an important voice in the Modernist movement in literature. His confidence was rewarded when Edith Sitwell invited him to edit her own literary magazine *Wheels*: an offer he gratefully accepted.

All that remained now was for him to secure a place at the one university he considered to be worthy of his talents – Oxford. After a long and anxious period of cramming Brian Howard was accepted for a place at Christ Church College, Oxford. When he learned that Harold Acton had already achieved a place at the same college, Brian wrote to him with his customary immodesty:

Do you realise, Harold . . . that you and I are going to have a rather famous career at Oxford? Already we have got way beyond the Oxford intellectuals. . . . At present I am looking forward, Harold, to an Oxford which, on the artistic side, shall be ruled by you and I together . . . as we ruled Eton!

From the first Brian Howard was captivated by Oxford: it offered him a stage for his performance as Brian Howard, Dandy, Aesthete and Modernist Poet. At Oxford, he was a peacock: he dressed flamboyantly and deliberately sought to shock the tweed-jacketed

17 Brian Howard as seen by an Oxford contemporary. This caricature first appeared in the University magazine, *The Cherwell*.

"hearties" and traditionalists who made up the majority of Oxford undergraduates at the time. He revelled in being thought "excessive" and "unwholesome": dandyism (of a specifically modern as opposed to 1890's kind) became a way of life to Brian.

If to some of his Oxford contemporaries he was a style-setter, to others he was a vain and arrogant poseur. Though he wished to be considered as an important voice in modern literature, his achievement was negligible. The early promise of his poetry never really came to anything: his verse was always far too ornate and over-written.

Somewhat bizarrely, Brian Howard cultivated the riding set, and spent a good deal of his time "huntin' and shootin'" with the young aristocrats who were idling their way through Oxford in the early Twenties. Evelyn Waugh records this in his autobiography, *A Little Learning*:

> . . . in the intensely snobbish era which immediately succeeded my own, he [Brian Howard] contrived to make himself more than the entertainer, the animator, almost the arbiter, of the easy-going aristocrats whom he set to reform in his romantic model, like the youthful Disraeli inspiring 'Young England'. 'Put your trust in the Lords' was the motto on the banner in his rooms on his birthday and there are many placid peers today who may ascribe most of their youthful fun to Brian.

Brian Howard was unashamedly a snob who delighted in the company of the rich and high-born. They could not quite make him out, but enjoyed his flamboyant, larger than life, personality.

Maurice Bowra in his book of reminiscences, *Memories 1898–1939*, has left us a vivid picture of Brian as an Oxford undergraduate:

> If Harold [Acton] was welcoming, Brian was aloof and self-contained. He spoke with marked mannerisms, emphasising each point as he made it and choosing his words for their unusual flavour, often with a hint of inverted commas when he dropped into colloquialisms. He addressed one frequently as 'my dear' and sought more to dominate than to please . . .

Brian Howard came down from Oxford in 1926 without a degree (something his father found difficult to forgive). Characteristically, he threw one final farewell party for 22 hand-picked guests, who were all sent invitations on thick cream card, 14 inches by 10, heavily printed in gold, instructing them to come wearing *robes de fantaisie*.

Brian Howard seemed to be in danger of living his whole life as though it was a *fantaisie*, as remote from reality as the parties he and his friends spent so much of their time devising and enjoying. It was at this time that the press "discovered" the Bright Young People, casting Brian Howard in the role of latterday Lord of Misrule, with some justice since he frequently was the instigator of their wilder behaviour. Brian and his friends responded with extrovert glee to the press's interest, and censure. Their antics became increasingly madcap and hilarious, or silly and juvenile (according to your point of view), as time went on. They delighted in causing mayhem and confusion. Martin Green in *The Children of The Sun* records some of their zanier escapades:

> Brian and his friends burgled other friends' houses, landed illegally on the islands in the lake at Wembley Fun Fairs, played leapfrog through Selfridges, set the Thames on fire with petrol . . . they organised hoaxes, like the Bruno Hat Exhibition of 1929, which introduced to the public a fake Modernist painter. Brian painted the pictures, Evelyn Waugh wrote the catalogue notes, Tom Mitford played Bruno Hat himself, and the party to launch it was held by Bryan and Diana Guinness.

And always the seemingly endless round of parties, to all of which Brian received an invitation – if he didn't the party couldn't be worth attending anyway. He rarely threw a party himself: the simple fact was that he could not afford to. He never succeeded in holding down any sort of job (not that he tried very hard) and what little money he earned came from one-off articles for magazines and journals. He mostly lived on what he could beg from his mother or his friends. During the latter part of the Twenties his life seemed to lack all purpose: it was a butterfly existence, superficial and aimless. Furthermore, he was drinking far too much and, on occasions, taking dope. It is clear from letters he wrote at the time that he recognized the futility and triviality of his life, but lacked the willpower to do anything about it. Moreover, he enjoyed the free and easy, live-for-the-moment, devil-may-care fecklessness of his lifestyle far too much to make any serious attempt to change it.

However, in 1927 he bowed to pressure from his increasingly anxious mother, who continued to hold the central place in his affections – and also the purse strings – and spent some months in Frankfurt being psychoanalyzed. For a time, on his return to England, he seemed to have discovered a new seriousness of purpose, but this did not last.

The last couple of years of the decade were, for the most part, a bad period in Brian Howard's life. His drinking got worse and the amount of promiscuous sex in which he indulged increased. He made sporadic attempts to pull himself together but it was clear that only a major reorientation of his whole approach to life could rescue him from himself. This came in the Thirties with his discovery, whilst a guest in Germany of the Mann family, of the full horror of what Adolf Hitler was doing in the name of the Third Reich. Almost overnight he was transformed into a vigorous anti-Fascist. Many of his friends, and all of his enemies, found the transformation so unlikely as to be absurd and, certainly, the old Adam never entirely died in Brian: the dandy aesthete lived on, somewhat uncomfortably, inside the socially committed left-wing apologist.

When the war finally came he spent a brief, unsatisfactory period working for M.I.5 and then joined the R.A.F., where he was employed as a desk clerk until 1944 when he was discharged on the grounds of ill health. It was all rather tawdry and inglorious, and he found solace, once again, in alcohol. The remainder of the Forties and the early Fifties saw a fairly steady decline both in his morale and his behaviour until, finally, in 1958, he committed suicide.

In 1968 Marie-Jacqueline Lancaster published a biography of Brian Howard. It was accurately subtitled "A Portrait of A Failure". It was a judgement that had tormented Brian Howard for the last 15 years of his life. In a letter to his mother he had written, after earlier commenting that he recognized that he frequently behaved "like an intolerable middle-aged child":

> Remember that in my heart I know how disappointing I am . . . how wretchedly, in a way, I've failed.

18 Bright Young Things in fancy dress with street-workers.

Noël Coward (1899–1973)

Noël Coward's career spanned more than half a century, during which time he was extravagantly praised and fiercely rebuked, loved and hated, worshipped and ignored. As an actor, a writer and a personality he attracted controversy throughout his life, but never more so than at the outset of his stage career in the 1920s. For many he was the living embodiment of the mood and spirit of the Twenties. As the novelist Stella Gibbons observes:

Noël seemed to incarnate the myth of the Twenties . . . gaiety, courage, pain concealed, amused malice.

Noël Coward had been bitten by the acting bug early. Precocious and self-confident to a fault, he had made his first stage appearance at the age of 12 in the unlikely role of Prince Mussel in a children's musical play called *The Goldfish*. From then on he had, throughout his teens, lived the life of an aspiring young actor, ingesting small doses of education and large doses of theatre, appearing frequently in plays directed by the famous actor-manager, Charles Hawtrey.

After a brief and inglorious spell in the army in 1918 – "one long exercise in futility" as he described it – Noël Coward passed from the ranks of unambitious soldiery to the ranks of keenly competitive professional actors. Whilst "resting" (the actor's euphemism for being out of work), he turned his hand to writing plays. In 1920 *I'll Leave It to You* became his first play to be professionally performed, first in Manchester and then in London. A second play, *The Young Idea*, followed in 1923. Both plays were praised but neither ran for very long.

In 1924, however, his first "strong" drama as he called it, created a theatrical sensation when it opened at a little-known theatre in Hampstead, the Everyman. The play was called *The Vortex*; its subject was the hitherto taboo problem of drug-addiction amongst the wealthy young. Noël Coward himself played the central role of Nicky Lancaster, a well-bred young man who has become a cocaine addict, and Lilian Braithwaite the part of his mother who has shocked her son by taking a lover. The first two acts of the play are essentially comedy scenes, liberally laced with witty dialogue, but the third act unleashes raw, powerful emotions which shocked and stunned audiences. As Stella Margetson in *The Long Party* comments:

19 Noël Coward, looking bright and sporty, in a publicity photograph from the Broadway production of his successful revue, *This Year of Grace*, 1929.

20 Noël Coward and Lilian Braithwaite in the notorious confrontation scene between drug-addict son and adulterous mother in the last act of *The Vortex* at the Everyman Theatre, London, in 1924.

The final, highly emotional confrontation between Lilian Braithwaite as the foolish, amorous mother and Noël Coward himself as her neurotic, drug-addicted son, a modern Hamlet and Queen Gertrude, sounded an authentic note of desperation behind the brittle gaiety of the younger generation and the bewildered uneasiness of the old.

After a brief run, to audiences crammed with celebrities and socialites (who were forced to sit on hard wooden chairs), the play transferred from the tiny ex-drill hall to the Royalty Theatre, where it ran for six months, once again to packed houses. The play and its author achieved overnight fame (and notoriety). The critics were sharply divided: some were profoundly shocked, others eulogized the play. One wrote: "It is an unwholesome, degenerate, immoral piece!" Another, James Agate, the most influential critic of the day, spoke for the majority, however, when he described the play as a piece that "shimmers with wit". Noël Coward as actor, playwright and personality had arrived!

Revelling in the publicity the play brought him, he shamelessly played to the gallery:

I would like the reporters to know that I have a dreadfully depraved mind!

The newspapermen, recognizing a supremely newsworthy personality, queued to interview him. He welcomed them with open arms . . .

No press interviewer, photographer or gossip/writer had to fight in order to see me, I was wide open to them all; smiling and burbling bright witticisms, giving my views on this and that . . . my opinion was asked for, and given, on current books and plays . . . I was photographed in every conceivable position . . .

On one occasion he allowed himself to be photographed in bed, dressed in a vividly coloured Chinese silk dressing gown. As the camera flashed he closed his eyes and the resulting photograph, published worldwide, made him look like a dope fiend in the last stages of addiction. Such publicity added to the public interest, fascination and, in some

21 The infamous "dope addict" photograph which, to Noël Coward's intense chagrin, was published all over the world in 1925.

instances, outrage. Sackfuls of letters from horrified self-appointed guardians of the nation's moral health arrived at his Ebury Street apartment: irate ex-colonels threatened to horsewhip him!

In 1925 he fanned the flames of controversy further when he produced a comedy called *Fallen Angels* which portrayed two rich, bored young wives (one of them the sexy and ebullient Tallulah Bankhead), getting progressively, and hysterically, drunk over dinner while waiting for the arrival of the handsome Frenchman with whom they have both had passionate affairs in the past. Throughout its long and successful run it attracted epithets such as "disgusting", "vile", "obscene", "filthy", "nauseating" and "vulgar" – though it seemed to be less the sex angle which caused the hostile reactions than the fact that two apparently well-brought up "ladies" of good society were seen to get drunk, in public as it were!

Throughout 1924–5 Noël Coward had also been hard at work writing much of the music and lyrics for a C.B. Cochran revue entitled *On With The Dance*, demonstrating a remarkable versatility and flexibility by also singing, dancing and acting in sketches in the show when it opened, only nine nights after *Fallen Angels*. *On With The Dance* was an immediate success and even won high praise from those who were slightly shocked by its daring approach. The song of the show was "Poor Little Rich Girl", the words of which revealed, as Stella Margetson comments, "his mocking insight into the feverish impulse behind the frivolity of his own generation".

Throughout this period, and on into the second half of the decade, Noël Coward was lionized by society hostesses, the rich, the famous and the titled, who tripped over each other's evening dresses in their eagerness to invite him to their parties.

You could hardly open a Society magazine without reading, either in the social gossip or in a caption under a photograph, 'and Mr. Noel Coward'. (Alan Jenkins, *The Twenties*)

He loved all the fuss and played to his audience but he was never entirely taken in by the superficial glitter of the socialites' world: he knew success to be notoriously fickle. And so, though enjoying a full and exceptionally active social life, he continued to work hard as writer, producer and performer.

In 1925 further success followed with his own production of *Hay Fever*, a comedy in the, by then, instantly recognizable Coward style; then in 1926 he embarked on a lengthy and largely successful tour of the United States, where *The Vortex* in particular was acclaimed wherever it was performed (except in Chicago, where it "died"). Returning to England he rested briefly, then set about producing first *Easy Virtue*, and then *The Queen Was In The Parlour*, two of his plays, which he had first produced on the American tour. Both played to good houses. Noël then allowed himself to be persuaded by Basil Dean, the well-known theatre director, to play the role of Lewis Dodd in his production of *The Constant Nymph*: after three weeks he collapsed from nervous exhaustion. Shortly afterwards he left for the United States, then went on to Hawaii where he gave way completely and was forced to rest. The months of enforced inactivity enabled him to take stock. In his autobiography, *Present Indicative*, he recollected his reflections at that disturbing time:

Too much had happened to me in too short a time. I had written too much, acted too much, and lived far too strenuously. This was the payoff; possibly, I thought, the full stop to my creative ability which I had strained and overworked beyond its strength. My talent or flair for formulating ideas and dressing them up with words was squeezed dry . . .

He returned to England early in 1927, having decided that the key to success and stability in the future lay in not dissipating his energies unnecessarily by a hectic social life. From that time onwards a single-minded commitment to work was to be the answer. Soon the creative juices that he had believed to be "squeezed dry" began to revitalize his writing. He spent some pleasant summer weeks writing a light comedy called *Home Chat* which he produced in October: it was not a great success, but he believed he had a trump card up his sleeve. This was his lavish production of *Sirocco*, a play he had written for the idol of the musical theatre of the Twenties, the actor/composer Ivor Novello. Unfortunately, things did not go according to plan – the play was a disaster. For the first time Noël Coward had to endure the indignity of watching one of his plays laughed, booed and hissed off the stage. Though deeply disappointed he quickly overcame his self-pity, and, determined to prove he could still produce a show of the highest quality. C. B. Cochran stood by him and entrusted him with writing the next Cochran revue – sketches, music and lyrics. He rose to the challenge and when it opened in 1928 *This Year of Grace* immediately attracted superlatives. Even the critics who had lambasted *Sirocco* and questioned Noël Coward's talent were forced to admit he had produced one of

22 Sonnie Hall and Jessie Matthews pictured singing the hit song "A Room with a View" on the front cover of a play souvenir of the London production of *This Year of Grace*, 1928.

the greatest revues of the decade. The show's two major hit songs were "Dance Little Lady" and "A Room With A View", which was played nine times at the Ascot Ball at the express request of the Prince of Wales.

In 1929 Noël Coward rounded off the decade by writing what was for him a quite new departure, a full-length romantic operetta, *Bitter Sweet*. His finger "on the pulse" of the times he had recognized that the public were ready for a change from the jazzy musicals of the Twenties: they wanted romantic escapism to help them forget their troubles. The show ran for almost two years, and was seen by close on one million people.

So the decade ended with Noël Coward in command: for ten years he had shocked, amused, irritated and entertained his audiences. His "snip-snap dialogue", as Stella Margetson calls it, had set a fashion which ever since has been associated with the Twenties. If, as Mrs Patrick Campbell said, his characters talked "like typewriting", it had become *de rigueur* for the Bright Young Things to abandon their aristocratic drawl for Noël Coward's clipped, staccato delivery. He had both reflected and created the style of his generation. Though he was to continue to do so in the Thirties, the Twenties had been, and still is in popular memory, "his" decade. As he observed himself:

Taken all in all the Twenties was a diverting and highly exciting decade in which to live and I wouldn't have missed it, not – as they say – for a King's Ransom.

23 Noël Coward arm in arm with C.B. Cochran, the impresario, his wife and a group of "Cochran girls" on Cochran's return from New York in 1928.

Nancy Cunard (1896–1965)

24 Lady Emerald (formerly Maud) Cunard, Nancy's mother, photographed by Cecil Beaton.

Nancy Clara Cunard was born on 10 March 1896, the daughter of Sir Bache Cunard, the grandson of the founder of the Cunard Shipping Line and his American wife, Lady Maud Cunard, who made it her chief aim in life to shine as a hostess and socialite, initially operating from her husband's country estate in rural Leicestershire. Petted and made much of by her mother's guests, Nancy lived a lonely, isolated existence when they were gone, under the charge of her governess and the 40 or so servants who looked after the upkeep of the house.

This sheltered, protected existence came to an end in 1911 when Lady Cunard, who had fallen in love with Thomas Beecham, the talented young orchestral conductor, moved to London to be near him, taking Nancy with her. Nancy, by then 15, was already starting to nurse a dislike for her mother which was, later in life, to develop into open hostility. She was sent abroad to finish her studies, and in Paris made her first contact with the bohemian world of the Latin Quarter.

During this time her mother was studiously and successfully making a reputation for herself as a leading society hostess. Nancy appeared to be content to behave as her mother expected her to behave, but underneath her surface compliance lay a discontent and rebelliousness of spirit which was to lead her to reject her mother's lifestyle. When, in 1914, she "came out" as a debutante and was presented at court it was clear that Nancy Cunard was not impressed by the social calendar, or its glittering occasions. As she records in her fragment of autobiography,

> . . . one ball succeeded another until there were three or four a week, and the faces of the revolving guardsmen seemed as silly as their vapid conversation among the hydrangeas at supper.

By way of relief from such conventional occasions, Nancy took to dressing unconventionally, and joining in with the bohemian lifestyle of some of her new-found friends. She was determined to live her life at full stretch. She was enthusiastic about all the "modern" literary and artistic fashions – she loved Epstein's sculpture, Stravinsky's music, Wyndham Lewis's *Blast*, Ezra Pound's poetry, the Russian ballet and American negro jazz.

At 18 she was something of a beauty, with a very distinctive "look" and style, and even more distinctive voice. As her friend Iris Tree recalled,

> She spoke in high piping notes, punctuated by odd stresses and pouncing exclamations of jubilance or rejection: "Ohh!", "Ahh!". The obstinate staccato "No!"

The novelist David Garnett wrote of her:

She was very slim with a skin as white as bleached almonds, the bluest eyes one has ever seen and very fair hair. She was marvellous.

Nancy wanted complete independence from her mother and marriage seemed the only way of achieving it. To everyone's amazement, she announced in early 1916 that she intended to marry Sydney Fairbairn, a handsome Etonian (of Australian descent), then serving as an officer in the Royal Bucks Hussars. The marriage proved disastrous. Nancy grew bored with her husband within months of the wedding and seemed relieved when he returned to the "Front".

Nancy spent the summer of 1918 in Oxfordshire sharing a house with a friend, Sybil Hart-Davis, and writing poetry. While there, she fell in love with a young officer home on leave, Peter Broughton Adderley. After a brief liaison, he returned to the trenches, and was killed. Nancy was heartbroken.

1919 was a restless year for Nancy. She told her husband she could no longer go on with their marriage, but with Peter Adderley dead she lacked any kind of focal point for her life and tended to avoid facing her inner emptiness by a hectic round of social engagements and parties, spiced with a number of brief, rather hectic flirtations.

The new decade brought a watershed in Nancy Cunard's life. In January 1920 she departed for Paris where she was to remain for much of the next 20 years of her life, though she frequently returned to London and remained very much part of the London scene for most of the Twenties. As Anne Chisholm, in her perceptive biography, *Nancy Cunard*, pertinently notes,

In England it was the time when the legend of the Twenties was being formed; and the legend of Nancy as an archetypal Twenties girl took shape simultaneously. Indeed, the style and behaviour of girls such as Nancy were a basic ingredient of Twenties mythology, both at the time and afterwards.

Nancy, for her part, enjoyed playing the role which such a mythology demanded of her. For many she was "the new kind of woman": independent, unconventional and free-living. Never exactly one of the Bright Young Things (by their heyday in the late Twenties she was in her thirties), she very much set a

25 American and British artists and writers were attracted to the Paris of the Twenties like moths to a candle-flame. They gathered to exchange gossip and news in sidewalk cafés like the American Bar.

trend in the early Twenties: she wore her hair and her skirts short, smoked and drank (in public as well as private) and flirted openly with a variety of men.

Both in Paris and in London Nancy created a stir, and she became an object of desire to a whole series of different personalities, among them the popular novelist Michael Arlen and Aldous Huxley, both of whom became infatuated by her and wrote her into their novels. What appealed to her about Paris was its vital and off-beat bohemian tradition. There was still a sense of adventure about living there; food and wine were cheap and every other person in the Latin Quarter seemed to be an artist or a writer.

Nancy took herself seriously as a poet. She was no mere dabbler: between 1921 and 1925 she brought out three volumes of poetry, *Outlaws* (1921), *Sublunary* (1923) and *Parallax* (1925), which were generally well-reviewed. Her style was somewhat stilted, and she employed too many archaisms for such Modernists as Ezra Pound, but, as Edgell Rickword, the *New Statesman*'s young reviewer, said of *Outlaws*, "One can feel the pulse of an original mind beating through a rather uncongenial medium." This is very much how her poems read today.

In Paris Nancy met many writers, poets and artists, amongst them the bizarre founder of the Dada movement, dedicated to the overthrow of order and reason in literature and art, Tristan Tzara. Through him she met the leaders of the Surrealist movement. On one of her visits to London she was persuaded to contribute an occasional "letter from Paris" by *Vogue* magazine, which she used to praise her new friends of the Dada and Surrealist movements, and whatever else took her fancy at the time.

Late in 1925 Nancy's father was taken seriously ill. She returned to England and was with him when he died. Before leaving for Paris, she detoured to Southampton to look for African masks, carvings and bracelets for which she had developed a passion. Soon she was to be seen wearing ivory bracelets all the way up her thin arms and wrists, and, in doing so, created an instant fashion in London. One newspaper columnist noted this at the time:

26 Nancy Cunard, photographed by Cecil Beaton, wearing her distinctive (and notorious) African bangles.

> Ivory shackles: one thing Nancy Cunard did while in London was to create a new fashion in ivory bracelets. Each time I saw her she was wearing three or four large bracelets, each of them extremely thick and two or three inches wide.

Back in Paris she almost immediately began a long and frequently stormy affair with the French poet Louis Aragon. Aragon was a founder member of the Surrealists, a group of poets and painters who shared the view that the origins of the creative impulse lay in the subconscious and the world of dreams. They took over from the Dadaists as France's leading avant-garde group.

During 1927 Nancy bought a house in the tiny Normandy village of La Chapelle-Réanville, called Le Puits Carré, where she entertained a whole stream of friends. Then, in 1928 she bought an old handpress from a retired American publisher who lived in Paris, and set about establishing her own private publishing house. Working alone with Louis Aragon, Nancy managed to produce three books in her first year. The work was hard and painstaking (with many problems) but the Hours Press produced its first book for sale, George Moore's *Perronin The Fool*, in June 1928.

To celebrate she and Louis Aragon went to Venice for a holiday, but their relationship began to founder: Aragon found his financial dependence on her increasingly humiliating, and on one occasion attempted suicide. He left for Paris leaving Nancy in Venice. There, one night, she was taken to dinner at the Hotel Luna where a group of Black American jazz musicians were playing. The pianist was Henry Crowder. Nancy became fascinated by him. When she left for Paris, she persuaded him to accompany her. In Paris Henry Crowder played nightly at the Plantation Club, and Nancy Cunard became a regular customer of the club, and an enthusiastic devotee of "Black jazz".

Soon Nancy Cunard and Henry Crowder were living together. As Anne Chisholm observes, each was introducing the other to a new world:

> Through her he was now meeting the rich, fashionable and intellectual and finding out what it was like to live among such people on a more or less equal footing. Meanwhile, Nancy through Crowder, was able to penetrate the seductive, raffish world of the blacks in Paris, where she met musicians, actors, boxers and dancers. (*Nancy Cunard*)

When news of Nancy's involvement with Henry Crowder filtered back to her mother she was deeply shocked and distressed: attitudes to sexual morality had become more liberal in the Twenties, but the old taboos remained just below the surface. It caused a breach between mother and daughter which never healed.

In the Thirties Nancy's interest in Black culture, and the Negro Cause deepened and widened: in 1935 she privately printed a huge anthology of Black art and writing called, simply, *Negro*. She joined the Communist party and supported the republican cause in the Spanish Civil War. She became a campaigner for "freedom" and "racial and political tolerance", though always with a left-wing edge to her words and deeds. In the Second World War she worked with the Free French in London.

She died in 1965, writing poetry and speaking out against any manifestation of bigotry, tyranny or Fascism that she saw, or believed she saw, almost to the last, though plagued by physical and mental ill-health. In Nancy Cunard the spirit of rebellion never died.

27 Nancy Cunard dancing with an unidentified Black jazz musician.

Literature And The Arts

The Twenties was a period of great ferment and change in the Arts, producing much that was innovative and experimental. Though the politically committed young writers of the Thirties criticized their immediate forerunners for naïvety and a preoccupation with form at the expense of content, the writers and artists of the Twenties, by breaking significantly with the traditions and approaches of the past, opened doors through which the succeeding generation was able to step.

The most influential poet of the Twenties was T.S. Eliot, an American by birth and upbringing, who had made London his adopted home: it was there he wrote the most daringly experimental poem of the decade. *The Waste Land*, first published in 1922, captured the mood of rootless disillusionment and cynical disenchantment which characterized the early post-war years. Though allusive and "difficult" it was a poem that spoke to, and for, the intellectual youth of Eliot's generation. Another, though less demanding, Modernist was Edith Sitwell, whose poetry experimented with bizarre and unusual rhythms, rhyme-schemes and verse forms: with her own individual brand of word-colour she sought to counter what she termed the "verbal deadness" of contemporary poetry.

The most experimental English novelist of the decade was Virginia Woolf, a leading member of the influential Bloomsbury Group, the literary brother/sisterhood which counted amongst its members the caustic essayist, Lytton Strachey, and the novelist E. M. Forster (who published his last, and greatest novel, *A Passage To India* in 1924). She adopted the method first used by James Joyce, the Irish novelist, in *Ulysses*, which came to be known as the "stream of consciousness" technique, in her novels of the Twenties, *Jacob's Room* (1922), *Mrs Dalloway* (1925), *To The Lighthouse* (1927) and *Orlando* (1928).

The two novelists who most effectively satirized the follies and excesses of the Bright Young People and their world were Aldous Huxley, and, towards the end of the decade, Evelyn Waugh. Cynical, witty, sharply perceptive and, at times, wickedly funny, Huxley, like Eliot, seemed to articulate his generation's disillusionment with the past, its discontent with the present, and its fears for the future.

Meanwhile, Britain's finest, most authoritative novelist/poet, D.H. Lawrence, lived abroad in self-imposed exile, never having forgiven his native country for what he considered the unfair treatment he, and his books, had received during the war years. His last novel, *Lady Chatterley's Lover*, was almost immediately banned when published in Britain in 1928.

In the world of the visual arts, Percy Wyndham Lewis, the prime mover in the Vorticist movement, continued to paint in his own idiosyncratic, fiercely individual style. The young generation of British artists, led by such painters as Ben Nicholson, looked chiefly to the Continent for inspiration, and a bewildering series of "isms" (Post-Impressionism, Cubism, Futurism, Expressionism, Dadaism, Surrealism) influenced their work before, during and after the Twenties. By far the most original, and most reviled as well as most critically acclaimed, sculptor of the period was Jacob Epstein, whose statue in Hyde Park, "Rima", was frequently tarred and feathered by scandalized art vandals, who saw in his work only monstrousness and ugliness, where others saw genius.

The British composers of the Twenties tended to go their own individual ways. Many were little influenced by the syncopated jazz rhythms found in the popular dance tunes of the time, preferring to look to their roots in British folk music (e.g. Gustav Holst and Ralph Vaughan Williams). Two young composers who were influenced by American jazz were Constant Lambert and, to a lesser extent, William Walton. One of Lambert's most memorable pieces, "Elegiac Blues for Piano", was written as a tribute to Florence Mills, the Black American blues singer who died tragically young. Arguably the most gifted was the songwriter Philip Heseltine (better known as Peter Warlock), who, plagued by fits of manic depression, gassed himself in his Chelsea flat in 1930.

Outside the world of the "serious" Arts but part of the overall Arts scene were the popular song-writers and novelists whose lyrics and books encapsulated the thoughts and feelings of hundreds of thousands of people who simply enjoyed a good tune or a good read, and who, lured by the potent seduction of "the silver screen" were beginning to flock to picture-houses in their thousands. The most widely-read novel of the decade was Michael Arlen's sophisticated melodrama, *The Green Hat*, which sold more than a million copies and brought him wealth and fame overnight.

Aldous Huxley (1894–1963)

28 Aldous Huxley, A portrait photograph by the celebrated photographer Hoppe.

Aldous Huxley was born at Laleham in Sussex on 26 July 1894 into a wealthy upper-middle-class family already rich in intellectual achievements. His grandfather, Thomas Henry Huxley, had been the most famous biological scientist of his day, and his mother was the grand-daughter of Matthew Arnold, and the sister of the Victorian popular novelist, Mrs Humphrey Ward.

Aldous Huxley's education followed the traditional pattern for an upper-middle-class boy: he went first to Hillside Preparatory School in 1903, and then on to Eton in 1908. A delicate, highly strung boy, he was ill-equipped to deal with the rough and tumble of boarding school, but like so many others he learned to endure it and take from the system what was useful to him. His formative years were deeply scarred by a series of tragedies that left emotional wounds which never fully healed. In 1908 his beloved mother died, in great pain. Then, in 1910, the 16-year-old Aldous contracted a severe eye disease, which partially blinded him for 18 months; finally, in 1914, his elder brother and idol, Noel Trevenen Huxley, after a series of academic and emotional failures, hanged himself.

Aldous graduated from Balliol College Oxford in 1916 (having been excused military service because of his eye condition) with a first class honours degree in English Literature. He immediately took a teaching post at

29 A view of Eton College. Huxley made a reluctant, and far from successful, schoolmaster.

Repton, and shortly afterwards moved on to Eton. Though greatly appreciated by boys of a literary persuasion (such as Brian Howard) Aldous Huxley was not a great success as a schoolmaster. His somewhat bizarre appearance (he was more than six feet four in height, extremely thin, and wore thick-glassed spectacles) made him an easy butt for schoolboy teasing. Harold Acton described him as resembling "a juvenile giraffe that had escaped from a zoo". Furthermore, his classroom discipline left much to be desired. The simple fact was that his heart was never in teaching: his ambition, from an early age, had been to become a writer. In February 1919, after less than two years as a full-time teacher, he resigned his post at Eton.

Aldous Huxley's name was not unknown in literary circles: by 1919 three volumes of his poetry had been published, and all had excited critical interest, but, quite clearly, poetry could never provide him with anything other than a meagre income. Knowing this, he set out to earn a living as a freelance writer.

In 1917 he had spent seven months at the home of Lady Ottoline Morrell, Garsington Manor, near Oxford. There he had met many of the leading writers and intellectuals of the day. Lady Ottoline admired his poetry (which was heavily influenced by the French Symbolist poets), liked him, and did all she could to further his career. She, and her friends, had also influenced his attitude to the war: Garsington Manor was a meeting place for pacifists and those opposed to the war, and Aldous Huxley was soon a passionate supporter of their views.

At Garsington he had also met Maria Nys, the beautiful and intelligent daughter of a refugee Belgian industrialist, with whom he fell in love. They were married on 10 July 1919.

Aldous Huxley was a man of wide-ranging and catholic interests, with an inquisitive mind which delighted in the acquisition of knowledge, however arcane or off-beat. Roy Campbell, the South African poet, with whom he shared a flat in London, recalls him holding forth on the unusual copulating methods employed by crayfish, and another friend records his fascination with the mechanism by which grasshoppers hop. His encyclopaedic knowledge of weird and wonderful phenomena became a standing joke to his friends, but he used it to good effect by writing on a whole range of subjects for a whole range of different magazines (including *Vogue* and *House and Garden*) in the early Twenties, making a living from it and buying himself time to pursue his true vocation, as a writer of "serious" literature.

By 1921 he had earned enough money to finance a trip to Italy with his wife and young son. It was the beginning of a lifetime's fascination with travel for the Huxleys. Fortunately, Maria shared both Aldous's detestation of the English climate and his preference for the pace of life of the Mediterranean countries.

While staying in Forte dei Marmi near Pisa Aldous wrote his first significant novel, *Crome Yellow*, which was published in November 1921. Set at a house party given by a literary society hostess at her country house, it was clearly based on his own experiences as a guest of Lady Ottoline Morrell. It was equally clear that a number of the book's central characters were based upon people he had met at Garsington, most obviously Bertrand Russell and Lady Ottoline, who appears as the rather absurd hostess of Crome. Both Russell and Lady Ottoline were extremely angry: Lady Ottoline in particular considered the book a breach of trust, an act of ingratitude and personally hurtful.

30 A front cover of the fashion magazine *Vogue*, designed by Benito in 1927. Huxley was a staff-writer for the magazine for six years.

Crome Yellow, however, was a great success: its glittering, cynical dialogue, recorded by the author with a gleeful, and at times mischievous, relish, and its cast of bizarre characters, found an instant readership in the young intelligentsia of the early Twenties, who greatly enjoyed Aldous Huxley's irreverent guying of the Garsington set.

Though most bought the book to be entertained by its wit and style, some recognized that beneath its surface frivolity lay a bleakly cynical view of life. The central characters in *Crome Yellow* may be absurd, but they are also pathetically inadequate human beings: escapists trying to hide the essential emptiness and fraudulence of their lives.

Throughout 1922 Aldous Huxley was infatuated with Nancy Cunard. He followed her about with dog-like devotion, paced dejectedly about the house waiting for her to telephone him, even turned up at her parties (which he hated). Nancy, for her part, found him companionable and a stimulating talker, but showed little interest in him as a lover: typically, she kept him dangling. Maria Huxley, believing that the fires of Aldous's passion for Nancy would soon die down, turned a blind eye to what was happening, until, in the summer of 1923, she decided enough was enough and issued an ultimatum. She told him she was leaving for Italy; he could either go with her or stay behind with Nancy. They left for Italy, together, on the following day.

During this period, and spurred on by the success of *Crome Yellow*, Aldous Huxley was hard at work on a second novel, *Antic Hay*, which was published in November 1923. This time his target was, primarily, the world of artistic bohemia and London's café society, whose denizens he portrayed as sterile and self-regarding hedonists engaged in a grotesque and futile social dance. Again, some of the central characters were clearly based upon living models, including Nancy Cunard, whom he was clearly trying to write out of his system.

Antic Hay added greatly to Aldous Huxley's reputation as a chronicler of the follies and excesses of the post-war generation: it also added greatly to his notoriety among certain sections of the popular press who, misunderstanding his satirical intent, accused him of glamorizing the lives of his sex-obsessed, frivolous characters.

In his next novel *These Barren Leaves*, written in the summer of 1924 and published in January 1925, he again turned to a variety of interconnecting love entanglements for his story. However, in the final pages of the book he sends his central character, Calamy, disillusioned by his life of trivial pleasure-seeking, off to a mountain retreat to learn spiritual awareness through contemplation and self-denial. (This was an attempt to answer his critics' complaint that his previous books had been essentially negative and destructive.)

Aldous Huxley had been fascinated and intrigued by eastern mysticism since his Oxford days, though he remained very much an agnostic so far as religion was concerned. Mysticism was one possible answer to the seeming futility of "modern" life. So, in September 1925, his bank balance now healthy, he set off on a round-the-world journey to

India, the Straits Settlements, Java, Hong Kong and America, returning ten months later in June 1926. Whilst journeying he kept a journal which enabled him to write an account of his trip, published in October 1926, under the title *Jesting Pilate*.

If Aldous Huxley had gone to India seeking Truth, *Jesting Pilate* testifies that he did not feel that he had found it. Though it strengthened and increased his interest in mysticism his experience of the realities of everyday life in India left him repelled by the squalor and miserable poverty of so many Indians. He wrote:

> One is all for religion until one visits a religious country. Then one is all for drains, machinery and the minimum wage.

Late in 1926, whilst on a trip to Florence, Aldous Huxley renewed his acquaintance with the expatriate English novelist and poet, D.H. Lawrence, whom he had first met in 1915 at Garsington and whose remarkable personality had made a strong impression on him.

In the early months of 1927 he worked on creating a character based on Lawrence, whom he saw as a genius. The novel, published in 1928, was called *Point Counter Point*. Lawrence himself was sceptical, and a little irritated. He found Rampion, the character based on him, something of a "gasbag" (which he did not consider himself to be), though he recognized that Huxley intended a compliment by his characterization. Furthermore, he admired the book, and wrote to Huxley:

> I have read 'Point Counter Point' with a heart sinking through my boot-soles and a rising admiration. I do think you've shown the truth, perhaps the last truth, about you and your generation, with really really fine courage.

Lawrence was not the only person to be used as a character-model in *Point Counter Point*, and Nancy Cunard appears once again as the rich, arrogant, promiscuous and destructive Lucy Tantamount.

As a picture of Huxley's muddled, rootless generation *Point Counter Point* is a *tour de force*, though critics continue to argue about its lasting merit. Lacking perhaps the wit and verve of his early novels, its darker undertones suggest a greater maturity of response to the dilemmas of the age. Aldous Huxley had at times been accused of being too aloof

31 Aldous and Maria Huxley with their son, Matthew.

and loftily disdainful of human weakness, but *Point Counter Point* made it clear that he was passionately, and personally, involved in the problems of his generation. It remains a dark, at times disquieting book, despite its moments of macabre comedy, and its seriousness of purpose cannot be doubted. With the writing of it Aldous Huxley believed he had come of age as a novelist, but he also felt that he had made his final satirical statement about the lives of his contemporaries. His next important novel, written three years later, in 1931, and not published until 1932, was *Brave New World*, which represented a new departure for him: a nightmarish look into a future in which humanity has been effectively destroyed by science. In the Thirties Aldous and Maria Huxley spent most of their time abroad, setting up home in the United States in 1937, and remaining there for the rest of their lives.

Aldous Huxley died of cancer in 1963.

Percy Wyndham Lewis (1882–1957)

Percy Wyndham Lewis was a maverick figure in the world of literature and the Arts in the Twenties (and the previous decade): a brilliant draughtsman and an original and experimental artist, he was also a novelist, essayist, critic, editor and man of ideas. Pugnaciously independent, quarrelsome and egotistic, he excited controversy throughout his life.

Born in Canada in 1882, he was educated at Rugby, where he achieved a reputation for laziness and rebelliousness. Disliking rules and authority, he was an uncomfortable Public schoolboy. In 1898, on the recommendation of his housemaster, he became a student at the Slade School of Art, where again he rapidly achieved the reputation of being a rebel who seemed temperamentally incapable of accepting established ideas or practices. After three difficult years he left to continue his education as an artist "on the pulses". His early twenties were spent on a series of bohemian adventures on the Continent, from which he returned in 1908.

The next few years saw him flexing the muscles of his imagination both as an artist and as a writer. In 1909 he met the young American expatriate poet and critic, Ezra Pound, who was busy stirring up the English literary scene with his controversial opinions and iconoclastic energy. The two men had much in common.

Pound did all he could to promote Lewis's work. He saw Lewis as an ideal champion for a rebel, break-away movement in contemporary art. Lewis had been one of the first painters in England to paint in the Cubist style and he was now developing an experimental style influenced by modern machine shapes. He seemed a natural leader: his truculent, abrasive personality coupled with his outsize ego and strong sense of his own rightness made him stand out as a figure to be reckoned with.

32 The Vorticists at the Restaurant de la tour Eiffel, spring 1915, by William Roberts. Wyndham Lewis, wearing his distinctive black sombrero, is seated in the centre of the painting. Seated nearest to the painter is Ezra Pound

In 1914 Lewis opened the Rebel Art Centre (its name aptly describes its intention) and in June he edited a brand new, original and experimental magazine called, simply, but accurately, *Blast*.

Blast, as its name suggests, was meant to explode upon the unsuspecting public, blowing away dead ideas and worn-out notions. It set out to shock, startle and stimulate. Everything about the magazine was arresting: printed on puce paper and using an innovative, imaginative typography and layout, *Blast* looked what it was, a brashly anarchic, iconoclastic kick at the culture of the day. Lewis filled the magazine with huge lists of people and things divided up between "blasts" (those who or that which should be "blasted") and "blesses" (those who or that which should be "blessed"). He also wrote a manifesto for it which proclaimed:

WE ONLY WANT THE WORLD TO LIVE, and to feel its crude energy flowing through us. . . .

'Blast' sets out to be an avenue for all those vivid and violent ideas that could reach the Public in no other way. . . . 'Blast' is created for this timeless, fundamental Artist that exists in everybody . . .

Blast lost money, but its impact on the world of British literature and art was enormous, and lasting. *Blast* was subtitled "The Review of The Great English Vortex", and was intended to be the mouthpiece for the group of artists and writers who had grouped themselves around Lewis and Pound, calling themselves, collectively, the "Vorticists". Pound had supplied the word "Vortex" which he described as that " . . . from which, and through which, and into which, ideas are constantly rushing".
As Jeffrey Meyers in his biography of Lewis *The Enemy* notes,

Vorticism tried to synthesise the innovative and iconoclastic aspects of Post-Impressionism, Expressionism, Cubism, Futurism and abstract painting . . . praised hard angular geometric art; combined primitivism and technology; . . . was fascinated with machinery, the city, energy and violence . . .

33 Wyndham Lewis's portrait of Nancy Cunard, painted in 1920, the year in which he had a brief, but passionate, affair with her.

However, before the movement could make much headway, violence of a more immediate and urgent kind overtook it with the outbreak of the First World War in the autumn of 1914.

Lewis saw active service on the Western Front and from late 1917 onwards was appointed as a war artist attached to the Canadian Army. In 1918 his father died, followed several months later by his mother. He approached the new decade feeling the cold wind of personal isolation. To add to his troubles his father had left him nothing in his will and throughout the Twenties and into the Thirties Lewis was hampered and humiliated by his lack of money.

In the early years of the Twenties Lewis survived mainly by painting portraits: the most famous, and arguably the most successful of these, was his portrait of Edith Sitwell. During the decade Lewis was a familiar figure in London literary and artistic circles. Less flamboyant and extrovert than he had been in his *Blast* days he nevertheless remained a striking personality. He befriended many leading literary and artistic luminaries and many of the young and talented writers and artists who were beginning to make their names in London and on the Continent. Among the latter were Ernest Hemingway, T.S. Eliot, the Sitwells (for a time), James Joyce and Nancy Cunard (with whom he had a torrid affair).

If Lewis sometimes showed a gift for friendship, he also had the knack of losing friends and making enemies. He could be, and frequently was, truculent and disobliging. Frustrated by his lack of money, and the need to find rich patrons, whom he alternately courted and reviled, he often spoke acidly of those who sought to help him. Eliot described him as "independent, outspoken and difficult". Others were less charitable.

In 1926 Lewis published *The Art of Being Ruled*, which set out to illustrate the isolation of the contemporary artist, and the need for men to create the kind of society necessary to foster and nurture the creative artist.

Though never a Fascist himself (a point which he frequently made) Lewis was clearly attracted by the seductive idea of a society led by a strong, benevolent "dictator" who could give to the arts its rightful place in society. Later this led him to praise Adolf Hitler at the beginning of his career as Chancellor of Germany in a book called simply *Hitler*. In the late Thirties he retracted this praise, but many people never forgot or forgave him, and this only served to increase his sense of isolation, real and imagined.

1927 was a key year in Wyndham Lewis's life: it was a year of solid achievement and some critical acclaim. He published *The Lion And The Fox*, a Machiavellian study of the role of the hero in Shakespeare's plays, in January; in February he published another new Arts magazine, entitled *Enemy* (something that he was increasingly feeling himself to be so far as London artistic circles were concerned); and in September his widely read and controversial study of the contemporary obsession with time, *Time and The Western Man*. Finally in November, a collection of experimental short stories based on his adventures in Brittany in his early twenties, *The Wild Body*, was published and well received.

It was a remarkable work-load for one man, but Lewis had developed into a compulsive writer: he seemed to have views on everything and to be determined to make his views known. A number of his friends were concerned about the effects, not only on his health but on the quality of his writing, of so much industry. T.S. Eliot wrote to him,

> I have felt for some time that it would be in your own interest to concentrate on one book at a time and not plan eight or ten at once.

THE "ENEMY" IS THE NOTORIOUS AUTHOR, PAINTER AND PUBLICIST, MR. WYNDHAM LEWIS. HE IS THE DIOGENES OF THE DAY: HE SITS LAUGHING IN THE MOUTH OF HIS TUB AND POURS FORTH HIS INVECTIVE UPON ALL PASSERS-BY, IRRESPECTIVE OF RACE, CREED, RANK OR PROFESSION, AND SEX. THIS PAPER, WHICH APPEARS OCCASIONALLY, IS THE PRINCIPAL VEHICLE OF HIS CRITICISM. FOR CONTENTS OF THIS ISSUE SEE BACK COVER.

WYNDHAM LEWIS
Editor.

THE ENEMY

34 *The Enemy* was Wyndham Lewis's third abrasive and controversial Arts periodical.

But Lewis was never very good at taking advice and was intolerant of criticism. He saw himself as a man capable of wearing many artistic and creative hats at once and he was aggressively proud of this:

> I am an artist . . . draughtsman, critic, politician, journalist, essayist, pamphleteer all rolled into one, like one of those portmanteau-men of the Italian Renaissance

Many found his arrogance impossible to stomach.

His answer to his critics was to write more books. In 1928 he published the first volume of a novel sequence, entitled *The Childermass*, which many consider to be one of his most original and challenging works. The scene of the book is a waste land outside Heaven where the "emigrant mass" of humanity awaits examination by the "Bailiff". It is a novel which anticipates by 40 years the Sixties' fascination with such science-fiction based fabular literature.

In 1929 he published *Paleface*, his last important book of the 1920s. In this he attacked writers whose work he considered "romantic" or subjective or sentimental or passionate: for him only reason, order and the classical values could fashion great art and literature. Yet Lewis could never tame his own passionate and stormy temperament. There was always too much anger in him, and of that anger was born bitterness, and at times, hatred.

In 1930 he published *The Apes of God*, a gigantic satire on the literary world of the time, dominated as it was by the Sitwells and the Bloomsbury Group. There is much comic gusto and extravagant, malicious teasing, but Lewis also launches into a vitriolic attack on the Sitwells, who are portrayed as posturing, narcissistic, pompous and self-admiring poseurs, bereft of talent or serious commitment to the true values of art. Not surprisingly the publication of the book caused a furore in the literary world. As far as the Bloomsbury writers and the Sitwells were concerned Lewis had put himself beyond the pale, and their ill-will was extremely damaging even to a writer of Lewis's reputation.

In the Thirties Lewis increasingly turned to his "political" polemical work for his satisfaction as a writer, though he continued to produce novels, and much of his very best painting was done during this decade, including his portrait of Ezra Pound (1938).

35 One of Wyndham Lewis's most successful portraits was of his friend, and fellow literary *enfant terrible*, the American poet, Ezra Pound.

Lewis spent the Second World War years in exile in Canada, lonely and unproductive, but returned to England in 1945. In the late Forties and the Fifties interest in Lewis's work was regenerated and his reputation largely restored. In 1954 he went blind, and he died in March 1957, one year after the Tate Gallery had held a large retrospective exhibition called "Wyndham Lewis and Vorticism".

Edith Sitwell (1887–1964)

Edith Sitwell was born at Scarborough, on 7 October 1887, the eldest of the three children of Sir George Reresby Sitwell, Bt and his wife Lady Ida. Her brothers, Osbert and Sacheverell, were born in 1892 and 1897 respectively. Her childhood, to which she constantly returned in her later poetry, was, by her own admission, a deeply unhappy

36 Wyndham Lewis's portrait of Edith Sitwell, painted in 1922.

one. Her father seems never to have got over the fact that his first child was not a boy and her mother, only 18 when Edith was born, was too concerned with her own petty frustrations to give her daughter the love she needed. The scars never healed. John Pearson in his biography of the Sitwells, *Façades*, comments perceptively:

> Edith's very early childhood clearly damaged her: she was to bear the mental scars of an unwanted child for life. The underlying self-doubts, the desperate shyness, the sense of being really both undesired and unloved would never leave her – nor would her morbid touchiness and her profound mistrust of human beings for the pain they could inflict on her.

If Edith Sitwell's later prickliness and sensitivity to criticism can be traced directly to her childhood unhappiness, so too can her sympathy for the outsider, the underdog, the lonely, the frightened and the persecuted. Though she could be a forbiddingly proud woman, she could also be a deeply compassionate one.

In her loneliness the young Edith turned to literature, and especially to poetry. In this she was encouraged by Helen Rootham, her governess from 1903, who was to become a lifelong friend. Helen Rootham's influence was not confined to Edith, as Osbert Sitwell remembers in his autobiography, *Laughter in the Next Room*,

> She was the first person we had ever met who had an artist's respect for the arts, that particular way of regarding them as all-important – much more important than wars or cataclysms, or even the joys of humanity.

It was to prove the basis of the Sitwell children's developing philosophy of life. When Osbert and Sacheverell were home from school they shared with Edith her enthusiasm and interests. Sacheverell was infected by Edith with the poetry bug:

37 Edith and Sacheverell Sitwell.

> When she wasn't writing poetry herself, she was reading it to me and encouraging me to write, so that poetry appeared a natural part of life. In those days Edith would have made anyone a poet.

Edith, Osbert and Sacheverell developed a camaraderie and fellow-feeling that was to endure throughout their lives.

In 1914 Edith moved into a small flat in Bayswater with Helen Rootham and during the war years she worked assiduously, and with a single-minded determination, at making a name for herself as a poet. In 1915 her first "slim volume" of poems was published, called *The Mother*, and in 1916 she edited and published an anthology of contemporary poetry, *Wheels*, which contained poems by

38 The front cover of the 1919 edition of Edith Sitwell's own poetry magazine, *Wheels*.

many of the young modernist poets of the day, including Aldous Huxley. Naturally, it also contained poems by Osbert, Sacheverell and Edith Sitwell. From the first, the Sitwells were to show themselves adept at self-publicity. Despite many setbacks, most of them financial, a *Wheels* anthology was published annually until 1921.

Edith was rapidly developing a poetic style of her own. Heavily influenced by the French Symbolists, she experimented freely with rhyme, metre and form, and what John Lehmann in *A Nest of Tigers* describes as

> . . . an extraordinary free association of images, drawn from classical and biblical mythology, fairy tales, nursery rhymes, historical reading and the poet's own childhood surroundings . . .

Her work was beginning to find an approving readership in literary circles, but it was the performance in June 1923 of *Façade*, a collaboration between Edith and the young, little-known composer William Walton who had been "adopted" by the Sitwells, which first brought Edith and her brothers to the notice of the general public.

Façade caused an instant furore: overnight the Sitwells, never averse to creating controversy, became living legends of the Twenties. *Façade* excited extreme reactions from audiences and critics alike. Its form of presentation invited parody: to the dance rhythms of Walton's atonal music (which included polkas, waltzes and foxtrots), Edith (hidden by a curtain to emphasize the impersonality of the poet) recited her words through a form of megaphone. Noël Coward wrote an irreverent send-up of the proceedings for his next revue, *London Calling*. It was a slight that took Edith 40 years to forgive. However much the critics and "philistines" (as Edith described her mockers) made fun of *Façade*, Edith and her brothers considered it to be an original, experimental piece, which fused the twin arts of poetry and music. They defended it resolutely in public and private. Later performances (more professionally managed and performed) bore out Edith's faith in the work and when revived in 1926 it was warmly received.

39 Edith Sitwell rehearsing with Neil Porter for the performance of *Façade* at the Chenil Galleries, London, in 1926.

Though the publicity surrounding the early performances had made the Sitwells look foolish and pretentious in some people's eyes it had also established them in the eyes of others as leaders of the avant-garde movement in the contemporary arts. Henceforward they were news. Though wounded by the torrent of critical invective hurled at them (especially Edith who was hypersensitive to what she called "gross public insult"), the Sitwells were not slow to capitalize on their fame or notoriety. They played up to their image as eccentric (but daring) "trail-blazers in the arts", in the novelist and literary editor Cyril Connolly's phrase, with obvious relish and gusto. For many people they represented an alternative set of values and views to the other group who set themselves up to be considered as arbiters of literary and artistic taste in the Twenties, the Bloomsbury Group.

Meeting the Sitwells could be a fascinating experience, as Loelia Ponsonby (later Duchess of Westminster) recalls in her memoirs:

> . . . it really was something to meet the Sitwells for the first time . . . they were so utterly unlike anybody else, and held a position in the arts that no-one aspires to today. The nearest, I

suppose, would be some very elevated, cultural pop-star, but they excited far more awe than any pop-star would . . . they were so extraordinarily clever and funny and there were three of them which made them still more disconcerting.

This image of the Sitwells was reinforced by the photographs taken of them by the gifted young photographer, Cecil Beaton, who was clearly fascinated both by their unusual and striking looks and the glamour which surrounded them in the popular imagination. He was especially struck by Edith's looks and appearance: where others saw oddness, he saw beauty. In his autobiography he describes her as she appeared to him:

. . . her etiolated, Gothic bones, her hands of ivory, the pointed, delicate nose, the amused deep-set eyes, and silken wisps of hair . . .

Edith was flattered, and Beaton was "taken up" by the Sitwells. His career rapidly prospered. The Sitwells' power and influence in the world of the arts was frequently used to foster youthful talent, and many young artists, writers and musicians owed their success to their encouragement and patronage.

Edith continued to write her own poetry. In 1923 she had published *Bucolic Comedies*; this was followed by further collections, *The Sleeping Beauty* (1924) and *Troy Park* (1925). All three books contained poems written mainly in an elegant, romantic vein which frequently hearkened back to the memories of her childhood which seemed to haunt her imagination. Perhaps her most successful poem of the early/mid Twenties was the long, concealed autobiography *Colonel Fantock*, which contained the following revealing passage,

But Dagobert and Peregrine and I
Were children then; we walked like shy gazelles
Among the music of the thin flower-bells.
And life still held some promise, – never ask
Of what, – but life seemed less a stranger then,
Than ever after in this cold existence.
I always was a little outside life –
And so the things we touch could comfort me;
I loved the shy dreams we could hear and see –
For I was like one dead, like a small ghost,
A little cold air wandering and lost.

In 1929 she astonished the literary world by publishing a long powerfully dramatic poem called *Gold Coast Customs*, which represented a major development in her poetic style. The poem's dramatic power impressed many who had formerly seen in Edith Sitwell only a minor poetic talent. The intensity and passionate energy, with the insistent drum-beat rhythm of its lines, vividly create an atmosphere of macabre horror and corruption:

Yet the time will come
To the heart's dark slum
When the rich man's gold and the rich man's wheat
Will grow in the street, that the starved may eat, –
And the sea of the rich will give up its dead –
And the last blood and fire from my side will be shed.
For the fires of God go marching on.

After the publication of *Gold Coast Customs*, Edith Sitwell all but abandoned poetry for the next ten years. In the Thirties she concentrated on a series of prose works and her only novel, *I Live Under A Black Sun* (1937). For much of the Thirties her poetry was unfashionable. F.R. Leavis, the Cambridge-based literary critic, made the much-quoted observation that she belonged "to the history of publicity rather than of poetry". However, in the war years she returned to poetry, producing poems which revealed a new, overtly religious seriousness.

In the last ten years or so of her life she continued to write poetry and prose, exploring, amongst other things, her fascination with the life and personality of Queen Elizabeth I in whom she saw a likeness to herself. Created a Dame in 1954, she greatly enjoyed playing the role of Grand Old Lady of English Poetry. She died on 9 December 1964.

Michael Arlen (1895–1956)

The most widely read best-seller of the Twenties was a novel which, with medodramatic flourish, set out to portray the fashions, foibles and follies of the Bright Young Things. *The Green Hat* was *the* book of the Twenties on both sides of the Atlantic, and its heroine, Iris Storm, the heroine of the age. Its author, Michael Arlen, became an overnight success. Selling more copies than any other book printed during the decade, *The Green Hat* made Michael Arlen into an instant celebrity; wealth and fame brought him social status, and he was rapidly "taken up" by London's fashionable hostesses.

What many found surprising on first meeting Michael Arlen was the discovery that (despite his English name) he was a Bulgarian-born Armenian. "Michael Arlen" was, in fact, the pseudonym of Dikran Kouyounidjan, the son of an Armenian merchant who had fled from Armenia at the height of the Turkish massacres and settled in Lancashire in the 1890s. There his business prospered and he was able to send his sons to an English public school (Malvern) to be educated in the manners and mores of the English gentleman. By the time Dikran left Malvern he used the epiglottal upper-class English accent with complete ease and assurance.

40 Michael Arlen at work on a manuscript in the study of his villa in Cannes, the Bella Vista.

Dikran was a very handsome young man: his sallow skin, jet black hair and attractively oval eyes made him popular with women of all ages and he was quick to take advantage of this.

After leaving Malvern, Dikran, at his father's behest, went on to Edinburgh University to study medicine but, after a mere three months as an undergraduate, he left Edinburgh for London to try to earn a living as a writer. At first times were hard for him: he lived in a small room above a shop in Shepherd's Market, scraping an income from journalism and book reviews.

Despite being short of money, Dikran was frequently to be found at the Café Royal, where he entertained beyond his means. There he met many of the young and aspiring artists, writers and musicians of the time, amongst them D.H. Lawrence, who took an instant liking to Dikran and invited him to stay on several occasions with Frieda and himself in Cornwall. There, Lawrence would offer him advice about the stories on which he was working. Influenced by Lawrence's advice, he wrote his first full-length work in 1920. Entitled *The London Venture* it was a collection of sketches, written in the first person, about a young Armenian (the narrator) called Dikran who is trying to achieve success in London. It was, quite openly, autobiographical.

The book was tepidly received, but for Dikran it was the important first step. On the advice of his publisher he had published the book under the name of "Michael Arlen".

In the early Twenties he had a passionate affair with Nancy Cunard which was to prove crucial to his development as a writer. His fascination with her led him to create heroines in his novels who were modelled on her (though many of the characteristics of his heroines would also fit many other young women of the time). She was also his introduction to the fashionable world of café society.

From about the spring of 1920 to the summer of 1921, Dikran and Nancy saw a great deal of each other. Dikran was clearly infatuated by her, and on one occasion even mentioned marriage. Nancy Cunard's recollection of the incident in her memoirs is revealing:

About now, the Baron [her pet name for Dikran] once said 'If I were rich, I should ask you to marry me – d'you see? But as I'm not, there seems no point in doing so – d'you see?' I did, quite apart from the fact that I was married and had not yet got my divorce, as I reminded him. The vanity of some men! Marry the Baron indeed!

"The Baron" was one of many young men (writers, artists, musicians) whom Nancy Cunard allowed to flutter around her like moths around a candle-flame: she enjoyed their company (and their devotion to her), but marriage was quite another matter.

Throughout the early years of the Twenties Dikran was writing furiously, determined to be recognized as a writer of popular appeal. His son, Michael J. Arlen, in his wonderfully evocative memoir of his father, *Exiles*, records:

. . . after the London Venture, he began to write like hell. The personal, alienated young Armenian of the sketches disappeared . . . Lots of short stories – about silly young Lords, who drink champagne in the morning, and marvelous new 1920's women, who swear (ever so slightly) in public, and are bored with the silly young Lords. The writing very mannered, in places wonderfully mannered, full of wit and elaboration, in places too full of curlicues and over-written. But something new.

Two sets of his short stories were published and three romantic (and more than a little melodramatic) novels. Then, at the age of 27, he wrote the novel which was to bring him

41 Michael Arlen, always immaculately groomed and dressed, was frequently to be seen wining and dining in the best London restaurants and night-clubs. His special favourite was the cosmopolitan Café Royal.

both fame and fortune: *The Green Hat*, written in a little over two months while visiting his parents in Manchester.

The Green Hat was a runaway best-seller at a time when the novel was in its heyday (and radio was still in its crackling infancy). Over-lushly written (Michael Arlen had a great love of the highflown phrase), it nevertheless captured the mood and spirit of its era with an almost painful accuracy. Its heroine – Iris Storm – had much of Nancy Cunard about her though she is far more conventional. The book created an image of England in the Twenties which both fascinated and repelled its contemporary readers, enabling them as Claud Cockburn, in *Bestseller*, observes to "have everything both ways". He goes on:

They [the readers of *The Green Hat*] could follow their guide, so gay, so debonair, with such an extravagant gift of the gab, through the brilliantly lit or darkly lurid premises of an imaginary aristocracy, identifying the agreeable with the beautiful, the high-born and the damned. And then, just as they might begin to feel some sense of guilt at their own enjoyment of the spectacle, the guide strips off his white tie and tails, grinds his frivolous . . . monocle under a stern heel, and reveals himself momentarily in the garb of a Minor Old English Prophet, rebuking the vanity of it all, and sonorously lamenting the passing of the Old Virtues, the Old Values and the Old Conventions.

THE ILLUSTRATED SPORTING AND DRAMATIC NEWS

DECRIED BY THE CRITICS: MICHAEL ARLEN'S "THE GREEN HAT."

NAPIER TAKES HIS WIFE WHEN HE GOES TO IRIS IN PARIS: THE CONVENT SCENE.

In the third act of Mr. Michael Arlen's play, at the Adelphi Theatre, Iris is lying dangerously ill in a convent in Paris and her doctor, despairing of her life, summons her former lover, Napier Harpenden, from England. Napier comes at once, bringing with him his wife, Venice, who witnesses the re-union of her husband with the woman who had always been such a powerful influence in his life. "The Green Hat," as is pointed out on another page of this issue, has been almost universally condemned by the leading critics, who have questioned its good taste and its effectiveness, but, as is well known, what displeases the Press often fascinates the public. Our picture shows Miss Barbara Dillon as Venice, while Mr. Leonard Upton and Miss Tallulah Bankhead are seen as the lovers.

42 A scene from the stage adaptation of *The Green Hat* in 1925, which starred the wild and wilful Tallulah Bankhead as Iris Storm.

The book was shamelessly modern and yet quaintly old-fashioned. It sold in its ten thousands, reprint following reprint. Michael Arlen found himself at the centre of the social stage, where previously he had been only peripheral to it. He was in his element. Dining with beautiful women, being seen with Noël Coward or sitting in the front stalls at fashionable first-nights, and attending all the most chic and smart parties, he was soon one of the most easily recognizable social figures in London. As Ethel Mannin remarks in her memoir *Young In The Twenties*,

. . . he was undoubtedly a handsome man in his Levantine [Indo-European] fashion, with his well-shaped head, his thick wavy dark hair, brushed back from a high forehead, the small moustache, and he was always very well groomed. He looked, really, what the author of a best-selling sophisticated novel could be expected to look like.

And he knew it. He played up to his image with panache: it was said that his white waistcoat always seemed to be whiter than anybody else's. He dressed with elegance and style, and though certainly vain he forestalled criticism by a delightful line in disarming self-mockery . . . describing himself as "every other inch a gentleman" or "a case of Pernicious Armenia".

The Twenties more or less invented the celebrity business, as his son observes, and Michael Arlen was one of its first "celebrities".

. . . I used to come in late and look over the scrapbooks that he, or his publisher, had kept of those years, the late Twenties. Reviews. Photographs. Newspaper stories. "Mr Michael Arlen has taken up golf." "Mr Michael Arlen has left for Biarritz." "Mr Michael Arlen is in St. Moritz." "Mr Michael Arlen has signed a contract with Cosmopolitan" which made him the highest paid short-story writer on either side of the Atlantic. . . . He was on one of the early covers of "Time". (*Exiles*)

Meanwhile, the money poured into his bank accounts. He bought a huge yellow Rolls Royce: all part of the image which he knew was helping to sell his book.

In 1928, holidaying in St Moritz, he met and fell in love with a beautiful and internationally aristocratic girl, the Countess Atalanta Mercati. They married and set up house in Cannes in a villa owned by the Mercati family. He continued to write, though financially there was no need for it, but his later novels were not successful – though *Lily Christine* (published in 1928) "about a girl", as Alan Jenkins comments, "who wore glasses at whom everyone made passes", was highly regarded by some readers. However, after the phenomenal success of *The Green Hat*, which was made into a play first, starring Tallulah Bankhead, and a film later, starring Greta Garbo, the rest of Michael Arlen's literary career was almost bound to be an anti-climax. He knew that the Twenties had been his heyday, the "time of his life", but he accepted its passing with

43 Michael Arlen and his wife relaxing in the drawing room of their Cannes villa.

typical dignity and grace, and even humour. In 1949 he told a New York reporter:

I was a flash in the pan in my twenties. I had a hell of a lot of fun being flashy, and there was, by the grace of God, a good deal of gold dust in the pan.

Naturally, he must have felt regret, and a private sadness (movingly described by his son in *Exiles*), but he knew that the success of *The Green Hat* could never be repeated. As Ethel Mannin comments,

He had the courage to fade out when his glittering world collapsed into the greyness of the Depression in the Thirties . . . (*Young in the Twenties*)

He continued to write books at fairly regular intervals throughout the Thirties, but they excited little interest, and one gets the feeling that he wrote more out of habit, and a desire to fill his time, than any wish to retain, or later restore, his popularity as a novelist.

In her memoirs Nancy Cunard recalls a conversation she had with "The Baron" in the early Twenties. She was criticizing him for writing such trivial and frivolous books, and remembers saying to him:

'Why can't you ever write something serious? You have a beautiful gift of observation; you work like hell . . . Yet you go on and on writing about Cocktails with a capital 'C' and ladies and gentlemen of Mayfair the likes of whom never existed. Couldn't you try your . . . hand at something serious, just for once?'

To which, he replied, smiling, "It wouldn't sell, d'you see?"

He died of cancer in 1956.

Morals And Social Attitudes

The Twenties saw a significant change in moral and social attitudes, particularly amongst the younger generation. In rejecting the standards and attitudes of their parents' generation the children of the Jazz Age went a long way towards creating a morality of their own which challenged many previously accepted norms of behaviour. The older generation, to the delight of their progeny, were suitably shocked by the liberated ideas and behaviour which characterized the Twenties: they were, in particular, horrified by what they considered to be the shameful self-display of the fashion-conscious young women of the post-war years.

James Douglas, that bastion of traditional morality, thundered, as early as 1920, in the *Sunday Express*,

> The war has profoundly disturbed the feminine mind . . . it has cast modesty to the winds. It has abandoned all its reserves and reticences. The vogue of the jazz dance is one symptom of this frenzy. The violent outbursts of vehement colours in feminine raiment is another . . . But the most alarming symptom is the absolutely brazen display of feminine charms . . . the tide of corruption flows more and more strongly every day. The decadent and degenerate poisons of Paris infect our fashions. The remedy is the lash of public opinion. It ought to be applied without delay.

To the intense relief of such traditionalists, a man equally concerned at the so-called decline in moral standards was appointed Home Secretary in 1924. Sir William Joynson-Hicks set out to do everything in his power to counter the dangerous advances of "the new morality", or immorality as he, and his supporters, considered it to be.

Nevertheless, despite the Home Secretary and his kindred spirits, the "new morality" made many converts. In 1925 Dora Black, the wife of the philosopher and mathematician, Bertrand Russell, himself a leading advocate of the "new morality", published *Hypatia*, described as "the handbook of advanced attitudes", which set out to articulate the modern woman's approach to life in general, and marriage in particular (which the author considered a contract of slavery for the vast majority of women). The book was widely read and discussed, as was Dr Marie Stopes' book defending modern approaches to birth control, *Married Love*. Though aimed at married women (Dr Stopes was firmly against pre-marital sexual relations), *Married Love* was freely available to any woman who wished to find out about birth control techniques, and knowledge about birth control methods led to a rapid increase in the number of women prepared to indulge in casual sex, or "free love" as it was frequently referred to both by its advocates and its detractors.

New translations of the works of Freud and Jung led to many people reassessing not only their attitudes to sex but to children and their education as well. A.S. Neill, the founder of the libertarian, child-centred school, Summerhill, was "discovered" by many of the freedom-loving young intellectuals of the day. His remarkable and challenging book *The Problem Child*, first published to little effect in 1915, was republished in 1925 and caused great interest and excitement in "advanced" circles. Bertrand Russell also pioneered child-centred education, opening a school of his own (along with his wife Dora) committed to educating children according to liberal and humane

44 When, in 1929, the vote was given to women over the age of 21 (as well as women over the age of 30) die-hard traditionalists predicted a trivialization of politics would ensue. The above advertisement aptly illustrates such a view.

principles. He also, throughout the decade, recorded his attitudes and opinions on all the great social and ethical issues of the day in newspapers, magazines and books, gaining a reputation as a radical "free-thinker".

Nancy Astor was typical of those who, whilst seeing good in many of the "modern" ideas current in the Twenties, remained essentially conservative in their basic attitudes. An eloquent and forceful advocate of greater opportunities for women and a fierce castigator of male chauvinism, she campaigned all her life for greater controls on the sale of alcohol and strongly opposed moves to liberalize the archaic divorce laws then in existence.

For many people the Twenties was a time of change and transition, full of new, and often challenging ideas and attitudes: some championed them, others attacked them, and the vast majority of people simply accepted those ideas they favoured and rejected those they did not find agreeable. In general, the further away from London one travelled the fewer changes of attitude one found: to a mill girl in Lancashire birth control meant "doing without" and smoking was something that factory chimneys did.

Sir William Joynson-Hicks (1865–1932)

Sir William Joynson-Hicks, nicknamed "Jix" by press and public alike, was Home Secretary for much of the decade (he was appointed to the post in 1924 and left office in 1929). By the time of his appointment he was 58, and it represented for him the final summation of what had been a stormy and controversial political career. "Jix" had never been hesitant about nailing his colours to the mast, and his colours were always true blue Tory. He was the voice of the shire counties and commuter-land at its most uncompromising.

Born in 1865 in Canterbury, the son of a well-to-do merchant, Henry Hicks, he was articled to a firm of London solicitors on leaving school in 1881 and was admitted as a solicitor in 1887. From the first he was concious of the need to make "the right contacts", and to further this aim he became a freemason. In 1890, at the tender age of 25, he was elected Master of his Lodge.

Over the next decade "Jix", determined to make a name for himself, working hard at his solicitor's practice to improve his social and financial position. In 1895 he met and married Grace Joynson, the 21-year-old daughter of a rich and successful Manchester silk-manufacturer, Richard Joynson. It was not long before he was taking full advantage of his father-in-law's influence in the Manchester social and political circles of the day. He began to take a personal interest in politics; like Richard Joynson, "Jix" was, from the first, a die-hard Tory of the old school, who looked to the days of mid-Victorian High Toryism as the golden age of British politics. "I still wear the reactionary frock-coat of the Victorian Tories," he was heard to announce proudly later in his career. Which he did, literally as well as symbolically, as contemporary photographs show.

By 1905 when the next general election came round William Joynson-Hicks (as he

45 "Jix" clearly at home in his Victorian frock coat, in the company of King George V.

now called himself, capitalizing on his father-in-law's name as well as his influence) found himself standing as the Conservative candidate for the North West Division of Manchester against the Tory-turned-Liberal Winston Churchill. Winston Churchill swept to a convincing victory, and "Jix" returned home to lick his wounds, and bide his time. It came more quickly than he may have expected when in 1908 Churchill was appointed to the Cabinet as President of the Board of Trade. In those days it was necessary for a by-election to be called in such a circumstance. This time "Jix" was determined to gain his revenge – and succeeded. Churchill was defeated.

"Jix" entered the House of Commons triumphantly some weeks later, to the unrestrained delight of the Tory benches who exulted in the humbling of Churchill. They were perhaps a little disconcerted when "Jix" in his maiden speech spoke with a pompous self-satisfaction which left many listeners staggered. From the first "Jix" displayed a gargantuan smugness which seemed to be immune to criticism. And there was plenty of it. A.G. Gardiner, a contemporary journalist, wrote a damning indictment of his intellectual shallowness and glib tongue:

He has a thoughtless fluency of speech . . . his mind responds to the short-sighted view and the popular expedient. He thinks not as a statesman, but as a talkative man in a suburban train who has just read the headlines in his favourite paper.

In 1910 he lost his seat in the general election but in March 1911 he was elected unopposed for Brentford at a by-election, and the voice of "Jix" was heard once again echoing loudly through the corridors of Westminster.

When the First World War broke out in 1914 "Jix" was in his element: in great demand at public meetings, he rose to ever new heights of patriotic zeal and fervour. Bellicose, jingoistic and simplistic in his view of the War (Britain was right and Germany wrong), he saw it as his duty to rally men to the flag, being, by then, too old for active service himself.

In 1919, rather to his discomfiture, "Jix" was created a baronet: there was a feeling in the party that he was being "put out to grass". "Jix", however, was determined to bounce back into the limelight. As Ronald Blythe in *The Age of Illusion* observes,

It was not in Jix's nature to give up, self-inquire or worry. He couldn't stay down – any more than a weighted Chinese doll can stay down.

He began the new decade by championing the action of General Dyer in commanding British troops to open fire on a crowd of unarmed Indian civilians in Amritsar, killing 379 people. The extreme right wing of the Tory party, Empire loyalists to a man, applauded his pluck in speaking out: most people were rather appalled.

In 1922 Lloyd George toppled from power, and with him his coalition government. For the first time since 1905 a purely Conservative government was elected to office, under the leadership of Andrew Bonar Law. "Jix" was confident of preferment. When it came it was, initially, disappointing, so "Jix", returning to his principle of making "good contacts", began to cultivate the good opinion of Stanley Baldwin, who seemed likely to succeed the seriously ill Bonar Law. In May Baldwin duly became Prime Minister, and "Jix" began to move quickly through the political ranks. Finally, in 1924, he was appointed Home Secretary.

"Jix" was delighted: his virtue had been recognized and rewarded with the Cabinet post he most coveted. A strict teetotaller and a fundamentalist Evangelical Christian, he considered himself ideally qualified to be the guardian of the nation's moral health.

Beaming cherubically from his still-boyish features, oblivious to criticism or complaint, secure in the certainty of his own rightness, "Jix" opened his campaign by making life as difficult as possible for the thousands of foreign nationals living in Britain, whom he suspected of, at the very least, Communist and subversive sympathies.

However, this was a diversion: the real target of "Jix's" Great Crusade was to be the moral laxity and sinful decadence of post-war Britain. Shocked by the spread of night-clubs in the capital, he determined to clean out what he described as "the social sewers of London". The wicked and the sinful would be brought to book. As Home Secretary he had the full authority of the law and D.O.R.A. (the Defence of The Realm Act) behind him, and an army of "moral soldiers" – the police – to do battle for him in his moral crusade.

Encouraged by "Jix" the police mounted a series of raids on clubs where it was known that after-hours drinking was permitted. Most were summarily closed down, only to open up somewhere else under a new name. The police fought a constant battle of wits with the club-owners and their clients, many of whom were rich and famous, and some influential. However, "Jix" was a determined adversary, and painstakingly persistent. In the end few clubs escaped his interdiction for long, and even Kate "Ma" Meyrick, the owner of the famous 43 Club, the Manhattan and the Silver Slipper (where the dance floor was made of glass), was finally brought to book and sent to Holloway for 15 months, for bribing a senior member of the Vice Squad. When she came out she was surrounded by a crowd of delighted Bright Young People, a further source of irritation and annoyance to "Jix", who chanted

Come all you birds
And sing a roundelay
Now Mrs Meyrick's
Out of Holloway.

"Jix", like Queen Victoria before him, was not amused.

As the Twenties wore on Jix became increasingly a figure of fun to the younger generation who saw him as an absurd anachronism, a meddling busybody determined to stop other people having fun – the only problem was that he had the power to do precisely that.

To "Jix" Britain in the Twenties was like a garden overrun with decadent and unwholesome weeds, and he was resolved to root them out. Amongst the most insidious weeds in the social garden were the writers, artists and intellectuals who, spreading dangerously modern notions, were polluting the minds of the impressionable. The soil needed to be tilled and re-sown with good Victorian seed. Examples would have to be made of errant artists, however famous.

46 Kate "Ma" Meyrick, the "Night-club Queen", celebrating her release from Holloway Jail, surrounded by a group of smiling well-wishers.

Throughout "Jix's" tenure of the Home Office prosecutions of writers and artists for producing "obscene" and "pornographic" material took place at fairly regular intervals, though the two most famous cases were reserved for the latter part of his "reign". In 1928 Radclyffe Hall's moving (if somewhat laboured) account of lesbian love, *The Well of Loneliness*, was brought to court and banned. Then, more significantly, in 1929, the final novel of D.H. Lawrence, acknowledged by his contemporaries to be England's finest living novelist (though he had lived abroad for most of the Twenties), *Lady Chatterley's Lover*, was also brought to court, and banned. This followed the seizure and confiscation of a copy of Lawrence's poems, *Pansies*, and the closing down of an exhibition of his paintings at the Warren Gallery.

To the intellectual he [Jix] was plain anathema. He was satirized, caricatured and campooned with a virulence rarely seen in the popular Press since the Regency. (Ronald Blythe, *The Age of Illusion*)

But to the journalists of such papers as the *Daily Mail* and the *Daily Express* he was a hero. His particular brand of respectable philistinism provided them with an excuse for being sensational while appearing to be moral at the same time. Whether applauded or derided, "Jix" simply went his own way, immovable in his prejudices.

In truth, "Jix" was temperamentally and philosophically opposed to change of any kind. A charitable view of him would be that, committed to the traditions of the past, he tempered the wilder excesses of "The Roaring Twenties" with his own sober and vigilant puritanism. However, many contemporaries took a less charitable view: to them he was a pompous, narrow-minded, Puritanical bigot with too little humility and too much power.

In the general election of 1929 the Conservatives were swept from office, to be replaced by a Labour administration. "Jix" did not stand for Parliament, and was created Viscount Brentford of Newich in Sussex. The "Jix" years were at an end, but so too were the Twenties. Soon the frivolity and excess of the Twenties would be replaced by the bitterness and depression of the Thirties. There was no need of a "Jix" to counsel self-restraint and sobriety. He died on 8 June 1932.

D. H. LAWRENCE SHOW RAIDED.

PICTURES SEIZED BY THE POLICE.

The Warren Gallery, in Maddox-street, W.1, where there is an exhibition of paintings by Mr. D. H. Lawrence, was raided by the police shortly after six o'clock last night.

The police were acting on a search warrant for pictures and books that were supposed to be indecent. A dozen pictures and some books were seized and taken to Marlborough-street Police Station. The proprietor of the galleries refused to make any statement.

Mr. D. H. Lawrence.

The seized pictures are all nudes, described by such titles as "Spring," "A Boccaccio Story," "Fight with an Amazon."

UNUSUAL GENIUS.

Mr. Lawrence's paintings, which have been variously criticised, are the latest production of his unusual genius to bring the authorities to censorial action. A novel, which he circulated privately from Florence, was banned by the Home Office a few months ago, and the manuscript of a poem of his was intercepted in the post from abroad early this year.

The following comments on the exhibition were made in the "Daily Express" on June 17:—

"Twenty-five paintings, signed Lorenzo, in oils and water-colours are on view, and in nearly all of them the human frame is shown in its most intimate details.

"The ugly composition, colouring, and drawing of these works make them repellent enough, but the subjects of some of them will compel most spectators to recoil with horror."

POLICE SEIZE 12 PAINTINGS

Works by D. H. Lawrence, the Novelist

GALLERY VISIT

Yard Men Remove Pictures to Police Station

Scotland Yard detectives last night seized about twelve paintings from the Warren Galleries in Maddox-street, W., about which complaints had been received.

They are the work of D. H. Lawrence, the novelist and artist.

It is understood that the police officers also took possession of a number of books.

The pictures have been on exhibition to the public for nearly three weeks.

It is understood that following a report received by the authorities the police yesterday secured a search warrant, and visited the building after it had been closed to the public. They spent some time on the premises.

The seized pictures with the books were placed in a motor-car waiting outside and removed to Great Marlborough-st. Station.

The seized pictures are all of them nudes, described by such titles as "Spring," "A Boccaccio Story," "Fight with an Amazon." In an introduction to the catalogue of the exhibition Mr. Lawrence states: English artists excel in landscapes—" which do not call up the more powerful responses of the human imagination, the sensual, passional responses."

Mr. Lawrence.

A volume of poems by D. H. Lawrence called "Pansies," which were seized by the Post Office while being sent from Italy, where Mr. Lawrence is at present living, to his literary agents in London, were subsequently released and have just been published.

The exhibition at the Warren Gallery has been visited by eight thousand people since it was opened on June 14.

Mr. Lawrence was born in Eastwood, Nottingham, in 1885, the son of a collier. Before becoming a novelist he was a school teacher.

He has published a number of novels, several volumes of poetry, and a number of other books.

His latest prose work, "Lady Chatterley's Lover," was privately printed in Florence, but its publication was banned in this country.

47 Facsimile of reports in the *Daily Mirror* and the *Daily Express* of the closure of the Warren Gallery exhibition of the paintings of D. H. Lawrence in the summer of 1929.

Marie Stopes (1880–1958)

Marie Stopes was born on 15 October 1880 in Edinburgh. Her parents, Henry and Charlotte Stopes were curiously matched; he was 28 on their wedding day but she was 39, a fact which Marie, in later life, concealed. Though a punctilious mother, Charlotte Stopes never achieved a loving relationship with either of her daughters (Marie and her younger sister, Winifred), being too inhibited to show love openly.

This was significant because until the age of 12 Marie was educated at home by her mother. Thereafter her education was entrusted first to St George's, Edinburgh, and then to the North London Collegiate, one of the best girls' schools in the capital. By the time she left she was accounted one of the Collegiate's star pupils.

Her intellectual flowering delighted her father with whom she shared a close and loving relationship. However, Marie Stopes was growing into a strong-willed and determined young woman and not even her father's advice would deter her from enrolling as a student in the Botany Department of University College London (then primarily a male preserve) rather than at one of the women's colleges attached to London University. Her reason was simple: the best teachers were to be found at University College.

She took her final BSc exam after only two years, passing with honours in both botany and geology. Her joy at this remarkable achievement was short-lived: on 5 December 1902 her father died of cancer, leaving Marie feeling lonely and isolated.

On 13 October 1903 she left London for Munich, to continue her studies at the Botanical Institute attached to Munich University where she became the first woman ever to achieve a doctorate in Botany. She was now Dr Marie Stopes. Returning to England she applied for a job at Manchester

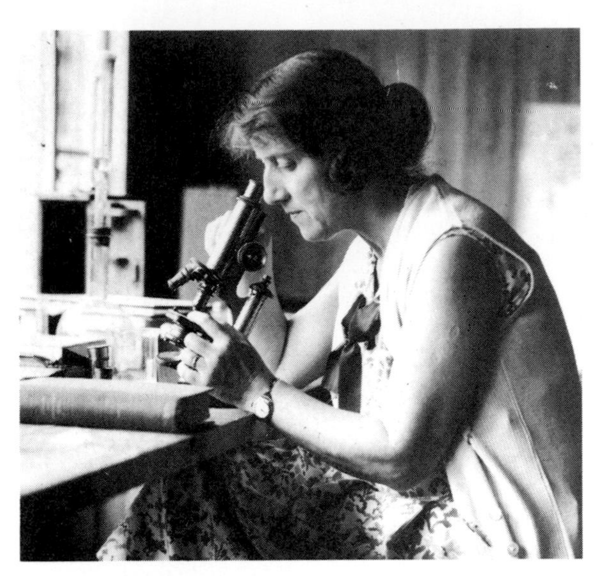

48 Marie Stopes at her microscope. She was one of the foremost palaeobotanists of her time.

University, as a junior lecturer and demonstrator in botany: to her surprise (the University had never appointed a woman to its scientific staff) she was accepted.

She was followed there by Kenjiro Fuyii a fellow botanist who had, despite being married, formed a deep attachment to Marie in Munich. She was not indifferent to him, but, equally, not prepared to make any sort of commitment. She was still wholly inexperienced about the physical side of love, but she was determined to discover the key to its mysteries. However, before this could happen, Fuyii returned to Japan, and Marie decided that she must find a way of joining him. So, early in 1907 she persuaded the Royal Society to award her a grant to go to Japan to study fossils of the earliest flowering plants.

When she arrived in Japan, however, she found, not an ardent lover, but a man whose ardour had cooled to such an extent that he even feigned serious illness to avoid her company. Marie was deeply hurt but she stayed on for 18 months, anaesthetizing her wounded feelings by intense study and research.

By the time she was 30, she was considered to be one of the most influential and knowledgeable palaeobotanists of her time, but her private life continued to be less than fulfilling. Then in 1911, while studying carboniferous flora in Canada, she met a handsome doctor, Reginald Gates, whom she married on 18 March 1911.

At 31, Marie Stopes seemed assured of her first sexual experience with a man. Yet the extraordinary fact is that when, five years later, she was divorced from Reginald Gates, she was still a virgin. During these years her professional career was going from strength to strength. However, the unhappiness of her married life was wearing her down and her health began to suffer. In May 1914 she left her husband and was finally granted a divorce in 1916 on the grounds of her husband's inability to consummate the marriage.

Marie Stopes' experiences during these years were to prove decisive. As Ruth Hall in her perceptive biography of her reflects,

> All reformers like to refer, in retrospect, to that particular episode in their lives when it suddenly became obvious what must be done to save humanity . . . the lifelong justification for her campaign for sexual reform . . . was the experience of her first marriage. The campaign later focussed on birth control, but began with a general concern for sexual education.

Marie Stopes was convinced that ignorance of sexual matters had blighted her marriage, and she determined to do her utmost to prevent this happening to others. *Married Love*, published in March 1918, was the book that made Marie Stopes name in the popular imagination. Till then she had been thought of as a brilliant woman botanist of slightly eccentric views and some literary pretensions (during the war years she had written no less than eight plays, plus a musical comedy, none of which were performed). After *Married Love* she was treated as an expert on a wide range of sexual matters – ironically since, at the time of the book's publication, Marie Stopes was still, at 37, without sexual experience.

Reading the book today the language employed by Marie Stopes seems flowery and effusive, but, in the context of its time, it was remarkable. At a time when most people still talked of a man's "rights" and a woman's "duties" Marie Stopes' book was heady stuff. Soon all London was talking about it: within a fortnight it had sold over 2000 copies; and by the end of the year was in its sixth edition. Marie Stopes was the most talked-about woman in London. But she was not married.

She remedied this situation in May 1918 when she married Humphrey Roe, the aviator, who had taken a great interest in her book, and, indeed, sponsored its publication. On her wedding night Marie Stopes finally lost her virginity: after that she was able to speak and write from experience.

On 18 November 1918 Marie Stopes published her second book in her new field of research, *Wise Parenthood*, a concise guide to contraceptive methods. Its essential message was clear. Marie Stopes did not pull her punches:

> On physiological, moral and religious grounds, I advocate the restrained and sacramental rhythmic performance of the marriage rite of physical union, throughout the whole married life, an act of supreme value in itself, separate and distinct from its value as a basis for the procreation of children.

To enable this to happen, birth control was not only advisable but essential, and, consequently, the facts about birth control had to be made public. *Wise Parenthood* added considerable fuel to the fires of debate triggered by *Married Love*. It was widely attacked, and widely read.

By 1920 Marie Stopes was rapidly becoming a household name. She was receiving a huge correspondence from a wide range of people (a disproportionately large number from clergymen and their wives), asking her questions about sexual response and seeking guidance with personal problems. Despite this, over the next few years Marie Stopes fought many bitter battles with both the Anglican and the Roman Catholic Churches. The press, very largely, was on the side of the Church.

Anxious to see her ideas put into practice,

49 The Marie Stopes Clinic in Whitfield Street, London, 1927.

in March 1921 Marie Stopes opened the first birth control clinic in Britain, in Holloway, a poor area of London. Consultations were free and contraceptives sold at cost price (in both instances to married women only) at "The Mothers' Clinic", as it was known.

Emboldened by her success, on 31 May 1921, she hired the Queen's Hall in London and organized a massive debate on the subject of birth control. Then in August she founded the Society for Constructive Birth Control and Radical Progress, and soon after published her own magazine *Birth Control News* to answer her critics.

By now not all the criticism of Marie Stopes was coming from her detractors, and those opposed to birth control. Mary Stocks (later Baroness Stocks), a strong believer in birth control, accused her of class bias, citing *Radiant Motherhood*, Marie Stopes' third book, published in 1920, as an example of this. As she pointed out tersely,

> . . . according to the regime set down in her latest book, motherhood is going to require a family income of at least a thousand a year in order to obtain the necessary degree of radiance.

The barb stuck: Marie Stopes knew there was much truth in it, however much she denied it. The fact was that though liber-

50 Overpopulation, leading to poverty and hardship, especially for children, was a social evil which Marie Stopes sought to limit through education in birth-control methods.

tarian and reforming in certain areas of her life and thought, in others she was extremely middle-class, conventional and even somewhat conservative. As a reformer she stopped far short of many radical thinkers of the time, insisting, for example, that only sex "within marriage" was permissible, and that abortion was morally wrong.

In 1923 she started libel proceedings against a Dr Halliday Sutherland. Though not in reality a "state trial of birth control" many people saw it as such and took great interest in its outcome. The jury's finding was ambiguous, but the Judge, Lord Hewart, who had frequently seemed biased against Marie Stopes, found in favour of the defendant. She immediately appealed against the decision, buoyed up by public support (even the press considered her unfairly treated), and Hewart's judgement was finally reversed in the Court of Appeal, in July 1923. It seemed to be a famous victory for Marie Stopes.

A month previously, her book *Contraception, Its Theory, History and Practice* had been published, and well received by the medical press. The trial, and the appeal, had given her, her ideas, and her books a vast amount of publicity. Now a household name she toured the country lecturing, and showing a film she had had made to illustrate her ideas called *Maisie's Marriage*. In November a play called *Our Ostriches*, written by Marie Stopes and advocating enlightened attitudes to birth control, opened at the Royal Court Theatre in London.

Then, during the winter of 1923, Marie recognized the signs of her own pregnancy and, on 27 March 1924, at the age of 42, she gave birth to a son, who quickly became the centre of her life. Her husband felt himself being pushed to the periphery, and their relationship deteriorated rapidly.

Still smarting from the indignity of his second round defeat Dr Halliday Sutherland had decided to appeal to the House of Lords. A national fund was set up, endorsed by the Roman Catholic Church. In November 1924 the appeal was heard by five Law Lords (three of whom were over 80 years of age), and they decided in favour of Dr Sutherland, with costs against Marie. Once again Marie Stopes was in the news, and once again she capitalized on it: publicity, good or bad, sold books, and her earnings from book sales enabled her to fund her enterprises.

During the mid-Twenties Marie Stopes devoted herself to the bringing up of her child, the furtherance of her clinic, and the promulgation of her ideas. In 1925 she published a study of her first 500 cases at the Clinic, and started training nurses in contraceptive techniques. She continued to travel widely on lecture tours, and her books were read all over the world. In 1927 the world's first travelling, horse-drawn birth control caravan-clinic took to the roads: it had enormous publicity value, though many women were afraid to be seen entering it.

In 1928 she published *Enduring Passion*, a book which she considered to be a sequel to *Married Love*. It emphasized the need for

> . . . lifelong love and enduring monogamic devotion, romantic in youth, rapturous in early marriage and matured in serene old age.

Ironically her own marriage seemed to be entering a terminal phase, though it dribbled on for a further 20 years, before Humphrey

Roe finally died after years of separation.

Throughout this time Marie Stopes was giving more of her time to furthering her literary ambitions – under a series of pseudonyms (designed to offset the by now risqué connotations of her own name). She wrote stage plays, children's stories, poetry and one novel, *Love's Creation*. Poetry increasingly occupied a special place in her life. But it was in the Twenties Marie Stopes had written all the important books for which she is still remembered. She had made birth control a subject which could be openly discussed. She lived on, prickly, argumentative, but ardent and determined to the end. She died on 2 October 1958.

51 Marie Stopes with a group of nurses from her mothers' clinic.

Bertrand Russell (1872–1970)

Bertrand (or "Bertie") Russell was born at Trelleck in Monmouthshire on 18 May 1872. By the time he was four years of age both his parents, and his infant sister, Rachel, were dead.

"Bertie" and his elder brother Frank, grew up under the austere regime of their grandmother, Lady Frances Russell, at Pembroke Lodge, the grounds of which abutted Richmond Park. Frank had already begun his education at Winchester College and he was allowed to remain there, but "Bertie" was educated by a series of governesses and tutors. He spent a lonely and isolated childhood, deprived of parental love and set apart from children of his own age. To add to his trials his grandmother insisted on his adherence to a spartan way of life. Not surprisingly the growing boy was driven in upon himself: he became an omnivorous reader of the books in his grandfather's exceptionally fine library; he worked with great intensity at his studies, and showed a particular aptitude for mathematics (the application of logic to the solving of problems gave him especial satisfaction).

By the time he had reached adolescence Bertrand Russell was beginning to recognize the price he was paying for his isolation and self-absorption. He recorded his thoughts and feelings in a secret, private journal (written in Greek characters and disguised as Greek exercises). On 9 March 1888 he writes:

52 Portrait of Bertrand Russell by Roger Fry, 1923.

I read an article in the 'Nineteenth Century' today about genius and madness . . . some few of the characteristics mentioned as denoting genius while showing a tendency to madness I believe I can discern in myself. . . . I should say it is quite possible I may develop more or less peculiarly if I am kept at home much longer.

His chance to "escape" came when he won a minor scholarship to Cambridge. His four years as a student at Cambridge were a watershed period of his life: it brought him out of himself and taught him to both enjoy and value the companionship of others. During this time he had fallen in love with Alys, a daughter of the American Quakers, Robert and Hannah Pearsall Smith. Despite family opposition, they were married in December 1894.

In 1895 Russell was elected to a fellowship at Trinity College, and between the years 1895 and 1909 his primary concern and principal preoccupation lay with his work as a mathematician/philosopher. Russell's marriage to Alys was under great strain throughout these years. In 1902 he realized he no longer loved her, and told her so. They continued to live together until 1911 when they separated.

That year he had a major love affair with Lady Ottoline Morrell, the aristocratic wife of Philip Morrell, the Liberal M.P. for South Oxfordshire. Lady Ottoline was, from the first, greatly attracted by him. She wrote in her diary:

Bertrand Russell is most fascinating. I don't think I have ever met anyone more attractive, but very alarming, so quick and clear-sighted, and supremely intellectual – cutting false and real asunder. Somebody called him 'The Day of Judgement'.

Their liaison was to continue for many years (their friendship for life), and change both their lives. Through Lady Ottoline, Russell came into contact with a whole range of important figures from the world of literature and the arts. For the first time he became aware of the narrowness of his own obsessive absorption in the life of the mind. In a letter to Lady Ottoline he wrote:

I feel so remote from the whole aesthetic side of life . . . a sort of logic machine warranted to destroy any idea that is not really very robust.

His relationship with Lady Ottoline, again in his own words, "liberated my imagination".

With the outbreak of War in 1914 Russell found himself a publicly controversial figure. He opposed the war. In 1915 he joined the pacifist No Conscription Fellowship and spoke and wrote eloquently in defence of the pacifist cause. In 1916 he was removed from his lectureship at Trinity, after he had been prosecuted (and fined £100) for writing a leaflet in defence of a young conscientious objector. By 1917 he was better known to the British public as a pacifist agitator than as a serious philosopher and academic.

Early in 1918 Russell was sentenced to six months in Brixton Jail for sedition. By the time he left prison, the war was over. Russell was out of a job, and cold-shouldered by many of his former friends.

For Russell, the Twenties, a new decade, opened with the old problems. His emotional life was in chaos. He was "in love" with at least three women: Ottoline Morrell was somewhat in the background, but in the foreground were the beautiful young actress Colette O'Neil, and Dora Black, whom he had first met in 1916.

In the summer of 1920 Russell received an invitation from the Chinese Lecture Association to give a year's course of lectures at Peking University. He accepted and Dora Black agreed to accompany him. After a fascinating and dramatic year (Russell almost died of severe pneumonia), they returned: Russell, as ever, to write a book, *The Problem of China*, and Dora Black to have his child. With the co-operation of Alys a divorce was hastily arranged, and on 27 September 1921 Russell married Dora Black.

Fatherhood had a profound effect on Russell: in many ways it "humanized" him. When, in 1923, Dora gave birth to their second child he was overjoyed, and deter-

53 Dora Black (as she then was) taking a photograph of Bertrand Russell during the year they spent together in China (1920–1).

mined to prove a loving and caring father to his children. His relationship with Dora and his children gave him a "new emotional centre".

Fatherhood imposed financial as well as parental responsibilities on Russell. By the early Twenties Bertrand Russell had achieved considerable notoriety: his pacifist stand in the First World War, his socialist politics and his atheist views, his deliberate flouting of convention by living with Dora Black before they were married – all combined to make him a controversial and unpopular figure. Yet, it was imperative for him to earn money. The only way he could keep financially afloat was to make use of his gift as a journalist and popularizer of ideas. Between 1922 and 1927 he wrote vast numbers of articles for a wide variety of magazines; he also produced a number of books designed to introduce the popular reader to areas of scientific thought generally considered beyond his or her understanding. The first of these was *The ABC of Atoms* (1923) in which he forecast that work on the structure of the atom would

> . . . ultimately be used for making more deadly explosives and projectiles than any yet invented.

This was followed by *Icarus or The Future of Science* (1924) in which he wrote, prophetically,

> I am compelled to fear that science will be used to promote the power of dominant groups rather than to make men happy . . . Icarus, having been taught to fly by his father Daedalus, was destroyed by his rashness. I fear that same fate may overtake the populations whom modern men of science have taught to fly.

In later life these prophecies were to become "the haunt and main region of his song".

In 1925 he published *The ABC of Relativity*, explaining the theories of modern physics, and brought out a new edition of *Principia Mathematica*, his magnum opus on the construction of a new foundation for mathematicians, written in collaboration with A.N. Whitehead while at Cambridge. He also published a book which encapsulated his thoughts on a wide range of subjects, entitled simply *What I Believe*.

During these years he was in great demand as a left-wing speaker: he spoke on politics, on the wider social question, on education, morals and religion. He stood for Parliament twice as the Labour candidate for Chelsea (in 1922 and 1923). On both occasions he was unsuccessful, as was Dora when she tried in 1924.

Russell knew that his serious philosophical thinking and writing was being, in Ronald Clark's phrase, "shunted into a siding", but

54 Bertrand Russell with Dora Russell and a group of her supporters on the steps of Chelsea Town Hall, the day she handed in her nomination papers as Labour candidate for the Chelsea Division, October 1924.

he was far too involved in the day to day business of earning a living and bringing up a family to care too deeply. In 1924 he bought a house at Carn Voel in Cornwall, and the Russell family spent as much time as they could there enjoying what was in some ways an idyllic existence.

Russell's interest in the education of his own children soon led him into a consideration of educational theory, and in 1926 he published a book which expounded the fruits of his thought: *On Education. Especially In Early Childhood.* In it he emphasized the need for a new approach to education: creativity in children should be stimulated, conformity discouraged; self-discipline should be encouraged; above all, he insisted that children should be given the freedom to develop.

However, it was one thing to expound a theory of education, quite another to see it put into practice. Russell, determined to do precisely this, opened his own school. The school, called Beacon Hill, was started in 1927 at Telegraph House (between Chichester and Petersfield), rented from his elder brother. There for five years he and Dora taught side by side until they separated: thereafter Dora continued on her own until her divorce from Russell in 1935 when she moved the school to Brentford in Essex.

Permanently short of money Russell was forced to continue writing his "pot-boilers" and articles for magazines. In 1924, 1927, 1929 (and 1931) he went on highly successful, and profitable, lecture tours of the United States. The proceeds of these tours not only kept the school solvent, but made him famous in America as a radical progressive thinker on education, politics, sexual freedom, marriage and divorce. Such indeed, by the end of the Twenties, was the reputation he had in Britain.

In 1929 he added to this by publishing

55 Bertrand and Dora Russell in happy mood with some of the children who attended their liberal/progressive school at Beacon Hill.

Marriage and Morals, arguing for greater permissiveness in attitudes to human sexuality, marriage and divorce. Among the points he made was that, in his view, complete fidelity was not to be expected in most marriages, but that a husband and wife ought to be able to remain friends in spite of affairs. In this both he and Dora certainly practised what he preached. In 1930 Dora Russell gave birth to a daughter by a young American, Griffin Barry, and a son by the same father two years later. Russell, meanwhile, pursued his own amatory adventures. In 1935 Dora and Bertrand Russell were finally divorced: he went on to marry his third wife in 1936 and his fourth in 1952.

Bertrand Russell's career from 1930 onwards would require a chapter to itself. Suffice it to say he lived on to the age of 98. In the latter years of his life he became world famous as a redoubtable campaigner for nuclear disarmament and was awarded the Nobel Prize for Literature in 1950.

Nancy Astor (1879–1964)

It is perhaps ironic that the first woman to be admitted as a Member to that most English of institutions, the House of Commons, should have been an American, but Nancy Astor had been born and bred in the staunchly Confederate state of Virginia in the "deep south" of the United States.

After a childhood of some privation, in her early adulthood Nancy enjoyed a life of considerable wealth and ease, her father having made a fortune in railway development and bought a large estate at Mirador near Charlottesville. In 1896, when she was 17, she was courted by the handsome polo-playing son of a rich Boston family, Robert Gould Shaw II. They were married in October 1897. After two days of their honeymoon Nancy left him and returned to Mirador. She had discovered Shaw was a drunkard. In February 1903 they were divorced, and the child of the marriage, Bobbie, remained with Nancy. Shortly after her divorce, Nancy embarked on her first trip to England. She took an instant liking to the country she was soon to adopt as her own. Later, she described

> this strange feeling of having come home, rather than having gone abroad.

A year later, in 1904, in the wake of the sudden death of her mother, Nancy returned. Profoundly distressed she sought distractions in the English social and hunting seasons. In 1905 she met Waldorf Astor, the eldest son of the expatriate American millionaire of German Jewish extraction, William Waldorf Astor.

Their marriage took place on 3 May 1906, and William Waldorf Astor's wedding present consisted of the magnificent mansion built by Charles Barry in the Italian Style in the mid-nineteenth century – Cliveden. Nancy threw her considerable energies into turning Cliveden into her own little kingdom, stamping her personality on to a

56 Nancy Astor, photographed in 1917.

house previously masculine and forbidding. Soon Cliveden house-parties were attracting a wide variety of guests, and Nancy was greatly admired as a hostess. For the time being she was contented. Waldorf, however, was not. Despite being plagued by ill health, he was determined to go into politics: an ambition which Nancy fully supported.

In 1911, assisted by his wife's spirited electioneering, Waldorf won the seat of Plymouth with a handsome majority. For the next few years, up to the outbreak of the First World War, Nancy concentrated on the bringing up of her four children.

In 1914, some months before the War began, an event of central significance to Nancy's life took place: she was converted to Christian Science, the movement which believed that sickness and disease should be cured by prayer rather than medicine. Her conversion gave Nancy's life a sense of direction, but it also served to reinforce her natural tendency to be intolerant of people and ideas she did not understand. Ironically, in view of her new-found suspicion of hospitals and orthodox medicine, when war broke out in 1914 Nancy found herself establishing a Canadian Red Cross Hospital at Cliveden in

57 Nancy Astor campaigning in typically vigorous style during the Plymouth election of 1919.

the almost ideal space created by covering the enormous indoor tennis court and bowling alley. Throughout the war years Nancy played an active part in the running of the hospital.

Waldorf, during this period, held a number of influential posts in Government, and his prospects for promotion looked excellent. However, in October 1919 his father, created Viscount Astor in 1916 against his son's wishes, died, and Waldorf's career in the Commons was abruptly terminated since in 1919 there was no legal method of resigning or refusing a hereditary title.

His local Conservative Association, determined to keep their Astor connection alive, immediately wrote to Nancy requesting her to stand as their candidate in the consequent by-election in her husband's place. Supported and encouraged by Waldorf she accepted and fought the election with gusto and determination.

She campaigned in her own, inimitable way. Driving about the constituency in a vividly decorated carriage and pair, driven by a liveried coachman, she stopped at street corners to harangue the passers-by. When somebody jibed at her "You're too rich to get the working men's vote!", she replied, "You'll see. It won't be seventeen thousand millionaires living on the Hoe who will elect me." Nancy Astor delivered a number of forceful election speeches. A quotation from one such speech captures her forthright style:

If you want an M.P. who will be a repetition of the 600 other M.P.s, don't vote for me. If you want a lawyer or a pacifist, don't elect me. If you can't get a fighting man, take a fighting woman.

They took her at her word and, on 28 November 1919 Nancy Astor was elected Conservative M.P. for the Sutton Constituency of Plymouth by a majority of more than 5000 votes over her nearest challenger, William Gay, the Labour candidate, of whom she had cheekily quipped, "Mr. Gay represents the shirking classes. I represent the working classes!"

When she took her seat in the House of Commons on 1 December 1919, history was made. She was introduced by the then Prime Minister, whose coalition government she supported, David Lloyd George, and the former Conservative Prime Minister, Arthur Balfour. Years later, she recollected, with characteristic humour,

I was introduced by Mr. Balfour and Mr. Lloyd George, men who had always been in favour of votes for women. But when I walked up the aisle of the House of Commons I felt that they were more nervous than I was, for I was deeply conscious of representing a cause, whereas I think

58 Nancy Astor, the first woman ever to take her seat in the "Mother of All Parliaments", escorted into the House of Commons by Arthur Balfour and David Lloyd George on 1 December 1919.

they were a little nervous of having let down the House of Commons by escorting the Cause into it.

It seemed appropriate that a new decade was about to begin: that the Twenties would open with a woman's voice being heard in the Mother of Parliaments for the first time. And Nancy lost no time in making her voice heard. Wearing her self-devised Parliamentary "uniform" (black coat, hat and skirt and white blouse) she was soon in the thick of things. Her aim was to speak for "the women and children throughout the country who cannot speak for themselves".

When, in 1920, there was a move to extend the grounds for divorce beyond adultery, Nancy opposed it vigorously, insisting that nothing should be done to undermine the stability of marriages.

I am not convinced that making divorce very easy really makes marriages more happy or makes happy marriages more possible.

It was, in many ways, a surprising stand for Nancy to take, being herself a divorcee, but, as ever, she spoke her mind, and her view was clear and simple: at all costs "the family" and "home" must be defended. In her view if divorce was made easier to obtain, the number of divorces would increase and the chief sufferers would be the children. Putting principle above personal consideration, she left herself vulnerable to her enemies, the chief of whom, Horatio Bottomley, was quick to take advantage of the fact that Waldorf had described his wife incorrectly in *Who's Who* as the "widow" of Robert Gould Shaw. He accused Nancy publicly of hypocrisy and deceit in his widely read paper, *John Bull*. For a while Nancy's position seemed precarious, her career threatened, but her supporters rallied to her defence, and, despite a number of ill-judged remarks and statements by Nancy herself, she won through, her reputation only slightly tarnished. Bottomley's campaign against the Astors continued but it was brought to an abrupt halt when he was arrested for fraud and given a seven-year jail sentence in 1922.

Throughout the Twenties Nancy campaigned energetically for causes in which she believed, whatever the strength of the opposition. With what Oswald Mosley once described as her combination of "unlimited effrontery and enormous charm" she made her presence felt in the House of Commons. As John Grigg points out:

. . . she did not seek to prove herself the equal of her male colleagues, since it was her line that women were the superior sex. 'I married beneath me,' she used to say, 'all women do!'

She campaigned vigorously for votes for women over the age of 21 (finally achieved in 1929), equal rights for women in the Civil Service, and the need to form and preserve a women's police force. She became a spokeswoman for the Royal Navy; spoke out against the evils of prostitution and brothel-keeping; and continued to warn against the evil of "demon drink". She campaigned tirelessly on behalf of children; she was one of the founders of the National Playing Fields Association which sought to provide recreational space and facilities for the young; she was a strong supporter of, and benefactress to, the nursery schools of Margaret MacMillan; she fought to counteract all forms of child abuse. To the embarrassment of some male M.P.s she even harangued them on the dangers of the spread of venereal disease. As she herself put it,

I don't know whether I have become a force in the House of Commons as much as a nuisance.

And, moreover, she thoroughly enjoyed being a "nuisance". Nancy Astor's achievement in the Commons in the Twenties was considerable. Her arrival and personal success opened the door to other women to enter Parliament (by the mid-Twenties there were 13 women M.P.s). She was a colourful pioneer and standard-bearer for the cause of women in politics. And yet she never quite consolidated her initial impact: something of its early promise was dissipated over the years. She was far too restless and impetuous, too uncompromising and idiosyncratic; also, having an essentially disorderly mind, she frequently muddled her listeners, and on occasions bored them when she was riding one of her favourite "hobbyhorses", such as her championing of the Temperance Cause. Though her fellow M.P.s frequently laughed with her, at times they laughed at her. In the 1930s she became a fervent believer in the policy of appeasement (conciliation with the German Fascist Dictator, Adolf Hitler) and Cliveden was frequently used as a meeting place for those politicians who shared her view.

With the coming of the War in 1939, and the fall of Neville Chamberlain, the idea of appeasement was clearly a dead letter, and its supporters were discredited. Though she helped make Winston Churchill Prime Minister in 1940, relations between them remained cool, and she was never given a post in his war-time government. In 1945, Waldorf persuaded her not to stand for re-election in the General Election which swept the Labour Party to victory, fearing she would lose her seat. She acquiesced to his view, but never wholly forgave him. Waldorf Astor died in September 1952. Nancy lived on into her eighty-fourth year. She died on 2 May 1964.

59 Nancy Astor loved to surround herself with celebrities. With her here are (left to right) Amy Johnson the aviator, Charlie Chaplin the filmstar, and George Bernard Shaw the renowned Irish playright and socialist.

Legacy Of The Twenties

Writing in her memoir of the Twenties *Young In The Twenties*, Ethel Mannin, the prolific novelist and essayist, records the contrasting and conflicting attitudes of the young people of The Jazz Age:

> I had forgotten until I looked at it again, over forty years later, that we who were young then, and who kicked our heels up to the Charleston, all but swooned at the tango, and charged about in the one-steps, were still occasionally critical of that very frivolity of which we were a part. There were over two million unemployed by then, and there were hunger marches. With a part of ourselves we cared, and with another part we were indifferent.

As the Twenties wore on, even the most determined revellers could not but be aware that something was seriously wrong in the state of Britain. The reality of the appalling social consequences of increasing unemployment was gradually born in on the minds of those who, living in the south of England, more specifically the Home Counties, had been cushioned from the impact of the slump in the fortunes of the old industries which had once made Britain a great industrial force in the Industrial Revolution. Lest they should forget, the unemployed, by the late Twenties, were reminding them sharply by marching from their cold homes in the North, to demand recognition of their sufferings and hardships. Ethel Mannin continues:

> The 1920s was a decade of paradoxes, of surface gaiety and hidden misery, of a generation dedicated to the pursuit of happiness in terms of sex freedom, and to good times in terms of cocktail parties, dancing night life, but all of it a gaudy superstructure imposed on the black, rotting foundation of the economic depression. London was one thing; industrial England another. It was two nations: two worlds.

In the late Twenties and early Thirties those two nations, those two worlds, began to meet, face to face, as the hunger marchers came in their increasing numbers to deliver their message of hopelessness and despair. The "haves" and the "have nots" eyed each other up, then returned to their respective lives: many of the "haves", their social consciences awakened, did all they could to alleviate the sufferings of the unemployed, but the problem was too intractable. Hastened by the Wall Street Crash in America (in October 1929) the European economies were sliding into a major industrial depression, and no one seemed to know what to do about it. Not even the Labour government of Ramsay MacDonald, elected in 1929, could offer any solutions, or even any hope. Bad as it was . . . it was going to get worse. And everyone knew it. By the time the Gay Twenties had given place to the Grim Thirties the dancing had stopped.

60 Desolation.

& LOVE

DATE LIST

1920 The League of Nations comes into being (10 January).
First public broadcasting station opened by Marconi (near Chelmsford).
King George V unveils the Cenotaph in Whitehall and the tomb of the Unknown Soldier in Westminster Abbey.
Oxford University admits women to degree courses.

1921 Proposed miners' strike collapses on "Black Friday" (15 April).
British Legion founded by Earl Haigh.
Marie Stopes opens her first birth control clinic at Holloway in London.
Education Act passed, regulating the working hours and conditions of work for children under 14.
Britain and Ireland sign peace treaty.

1922 British Broadcasting Company makes first regular broadcasts on sound radio.
The first Austin "7"s appear.
The first woman barrister called to the Bar (Lucy Williams).
Bonar Law (Conservative) replaces Lloyd George (Liberal Coalition) as Prime Minister after general election (15 November).
Irish Free State (Eire) created.

1923 Bonar Law resigns (ill health), replaced by Stanley Baldwin as Prime Minister.
Conservatives returned to government in general election.
First F.A. Cup Final played at Wembley Stadium (winners: Bolton Wanderers).
Baldwin calls general election, but fails to get overall majority and resigns.
First Labour government formed with Ramsay MacDonald as Prime Minister (November).

1924 British Empire Exhibition opens at Wembley (23 April).
British Imperial Airways founded.
The Green Hat published.
The Vortex by Noël Coward first performed.
After the revelation of the Zinoviev Letter (later proved to be bogus), the Labour government falls and the Conservatives return to power (29 October).

1925 The Pensions Act passed; pensions henceforward provided for the elderly, widows and orphans.
Britain returns to the Gold Standard (April).
First traffic lights installed in London.

1926 The General Strike (3–12 May).
Coal Mines Act, establishing 8-hour working day.
The Central Electricity Board created.
Imperial Conference in London (19 October–18 November); Britain and the Dominions declared to be autonomous nations of equal status.
The adoption of children legalized.

1927 Trade Disputes Act passed, making general strikes illegal.
British Broadcasting Corporation (formerly Company) established by royal charter.
Britain severs diplomatic relations with the U.S.S.R. (27 May).
First automatic telephones in London.

1928 "Flapper Vote" given to women over 21 (previously over 30).
Penicillin discovered by Sir Alexander Fleming.
First "talkies" (sound films) shown in British picture houses.
Mersey tunnel completed.

1929 Hunger march of unemployed workers from Glasgow to London.
B.B.C. begins experimental television programmes.
Baldwin's government resigns after losing general election (May); the second Labour government comes into office (Ramsay MacDonald again Prime Minister).
First English woman Cabinet minister (Miss Margaret Bondfield) appointed Minister of Labour.
"The Wall Street Crash" (28 October).
New York Stock Exchange collapses, setting off a worldwide depression.

1930 Britain, the United States, Japan and France sign treaty on naval disarmament (April).
Housing Act (Greenwood's) passed: problems of slum clearance tackled.
The Simons report on India recommends greater Indian participation in government.
Unemployment reaches 2½ million (December).

Books For Further Reading

General

Leslie Bailey, *Leslie Bailey's BBC Scrapbook*, Allen & Watson

Richard Bennet, *A Picture of the Twenties*, Vista

Ronald Blythe, *The Age of Illusion*, Hamish Hamilton/OUP

* Susanne Everett, *London: The Glamour Years, 1919–1939*, Bison

Robert Graves & Alan Hodge, *The Long Weekend*, Hutchinson

* Alan Jenkins, *The Twenties*, Heinemann

James Macmillan, *The Way It Was*, William Kimber

Stella Margetson, *The Long Party*, Gordon & Cremonesi

Arthur Marwick, *Britain in our Century*, Thames & Hudson

John Montgomery, *The Twenties*, Allen & Unwin

Cecil Roberts, *The Bright Twenties*, Hodder & Stoughton

Julian Symons, *The General Strike*, Cresset Press

Marina Warner, *The Crack in the Teacup*, André Deutsch

Angus Wilson, *For Whom the Cloche Tolls*, Granada

* Marion Yass, *Britain Between the World Wars*, Wayland

Individual Biography

The Prince of Wales

Ursula Bloom, *The Duke of Windsor*, Robert Hale

Frances Donaldson, *Edward VIII*, Weidenfeld & Nicholson/Lippincott

* Frances Donaldson, *Edward VIII: The Road to Abdication* (abridged and illustrated version of above)

Robert Gray & Jane Oliver, *Edward VIII, The Man We Lost. A Pictorial Study*, Compton Press

Brian Howard

Martin Green, *Children of the Sun*, Constable

Marie-Jacqueline Lancaster (ed.), *Brian Howard: Portrait of a Failure*, Blond

Noël Coward

* Charles Castle, *Noël*, Allen/Abacus

Noël Coward, *Autobiography*, Methuen (containing both *Present Indicative* and *Future Indefinite*)

Cole Lesley, *The Life of Noël Coward*, Penguin

* Cole Lesley, Graham Payn & Sheridan Morley, *Noël Coward and his Friends*, Weidenfeld & Nicholson

Sheridan Morley, *A Talent to Amuse*, Heinemann

Nancy Cunard

Anne Chisholm, *Nancy Cunard*, Sidgwick & Jackson

Daphne Fielding, *Emerald and Nancy: Lady Cunard and her Daughter*, Eyre & Spottiswoode

Aldous Huxley

Sybille Bedford, *Aldous Huxley: A Biography in 2 Volumes*, Chatto & Windus

Ronald W. Clark, *The Huxleys*, Heinemann

Grover Smith (ed.), *Letters of Aldous Huxley*, Chatto & Windus

Percy Wyndham Lewis

Jeffrey Meyers, *The Enemy: A Biography of Wyndham Lewis*, Routledge & Kegan Paul

Percy Wyndham Lewis, *Blasting and Bombardiering* (autobiography), Calder & Boyars

Edith Sitwell

Geoffrey Elborn, *Edith Sitwell: A Biography*, Sheldon

Victoria Glendinning, *Edith Sitwell: A Unicorn among Lions*, Weidenfeld & Nicholson/Oxford University Press

John & Derek Parker, *Selected Letters of Edith Sitwell*, Macmillan

John Pearson, *Façades*, Macmillan (a study of Edith, Osbert and Sacheverell Sitwell)

Elizabeth Salter, *Edith Sitwell*, Oresko Books

Osbert Sitwell, *Left Hand, Right Hand*, Penguin

Michael Arlen

Michael J. Arlen, *Exiles/Passage to Ararat*, Penguin

Sir William Joynson Hicks ("Jix")
Ronald Blythe, chapter in *The Age of Illusion*, Hamish Hamilton/Oxford University Press

Marie Stopes
Ruth Hall, *Marie Stopes: A Biography*, Deutsch/Virago
Harry Verdon Stopes-Roe & Ian Scott, *Marie Stopes and Birth Control*, Priory Press

Bertrand Russell
Ronald W. Clark, *The Life of Bertrand Russell*, Jonathan Cape and Weidenfeld & Nicholson
* Ronald Clark, *Bertrand Russell and His World*, Thames & Hudson
The Autobiography of Bertrand Russell in 3 Volumes (1872–1914, 1914–1944, 1944–1967), George Allen & Unwin
Dora Russell, *The Tamarisk Tree* (Vol. 1), Virago

Nancy (Lady) Astor
* John Grigg, *Nancy Astor: A Lady Unashamed*, Little Brown
Anthony Masters, *Nancy Astor*, Weidenfeld & Nicholson
Christopher Sykes, *Nancy: The Life of Lady Astor*, Collins

General Reminiscences of the Twenties
Harold Acton, *Memoirs of an Aesthete*, Methuen
Harold Acton, *More Memoirs of an Aesthete*, Methuen
Cecil Beaton, *The Wandering Years*, Weidenfeld & Nicholson
Charles Graves, *The Bad Old Days*, Faber & Faber
Ethel Mannin, *Young in the Twenties*, Hutchinson
Beverley Nichols, *The Sweet and Twenties*, Weidenfeld & Nicholson

Novels about the Twenties (written during the Twenties)
Michael Arlen, *The Green Hat*, Boydell
E.F. Benson, the *Lucia* series of novels, Black Swan
Aldous Huxley, *Antic Hay; Crome Yellow; Point Counter Point*, Penguin/Granada
Evelyn Waugh, *Decline and Fall; Vile Bodies; Brideshead Revisited*, Penguin

* Books marked with * contain a large number of illustrations.

INDEX